There's a Time and a Place

There's a Time and a Place

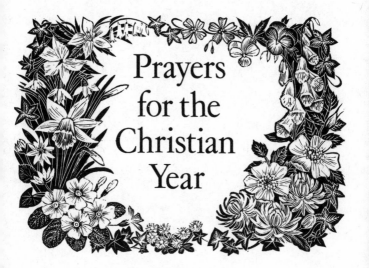

Prayers
for the
Christian
Year

Jamie Wallace

COLLINS

Collins Liturgical Publications
187 Piccadilly, London W1V 9DA

First published 1982
© 1982 text S. J. Wallace
© Illustrations 1982 William Collins Sons & Co Ltd

ISBN 0 00 599697 X

Chapter head illustrations by Yvonne Skargon
Typographical design by Colin Reed
Photoset by Rowland Phototypesetting Ltd,
Bury St Edmunds, Suffolk
Made and printed by William Collins Sons & Co, Glasgow

CONTENTS

For
Doris Tarplett,
Edgar Bonsall,
and Don Gocke
who were in the right places
at the right times

ACKNOWLEDGEMENTS

Thanks are due

to the Baptist Union of Great Britain and Ireland for permission to include each section's theme prayer: the ten
prayers appear in substantially the same form in the 1981
denominational prayer cycle *God Gives Growth*, edited by
R. Alastair Campbell; also for the prayers for Mothering
Sunday, which were originally composed for a Department of
Mission working paper on family life, and were used in a
broadcast service of Infant Dedication, Epiphany Sunday
1980; also for the Statement of Faith (p. 141), which was
composed for the closing session of the Baptist Union
Assembly, 1978; and for their Department of Ministry's sab-
batical leave scheme, which, together with Dr. Williams's
Trust, helped to provide the leisure for compiling *There's a
Time and a Place*.

to the editor of *The Baptist Times*, who commissioned the set of
five short prayers numbered Lent 7, to accompany a study
series on 1 Peter by R. E. O. White early in 1981.

to the editor of *The Fraternal*, magazine of the Baptist Ministers'
Fellowship, whose March 1978 number contained the prayers
for Whit Sunday morning and evening, Pentecost 3 and 7.

to the British and Foreign Bible Society for permission to
quote scripture texts from *Good News Bible* published by the
Bible Societies/Collins, © American Bible Society 1976.

INTRODUCTION

About the Prayers

These prayers could be called 'private and public'. They were prepared for church services, but I had prayed them before a congregation used them. Some of them were used afterwards in smaller groups, at home and in conferences; in a small group they can be read very slowly with plenty of time to think. A few prayers have found their way into classrooms.

This may mean there is a time and a place for them in school worship, in a house group or for family prayer, as well as in personal devotion and at church. In each of those situations, words borrowed from other people have often helped me; it would be nice if my words could help someone else.

Prayer, like the Church, is God's gift not our invention; neither the existence of the Church nor the practice of prayer is possible without the Holy Spirit working in us. So it may be that words for prayer which occur to any one of us are things which, like the early Christians, we should 'hold in common'.

These are 'prayers for the Christian year'. I am one of those people for whom using the Church calendar as an annual living-through of the salvation story, is an important and exciting part of Christian experience. Each prayer in *There's a Time and a Place* began as a meditation in the scriptures to which, festival by festival, the events of that story point us.

Using the prayers

These are all prayers to which I have returned more than once: sometimes to use them again as they stood, sometimes to adapt them, sometimes taking from them as a starting point no more than an evocative phrase or an undeveloped thought. It is as a resource to be drawn upon in this free and varied way that I hope *There's a Time and a Place* may prove useful to other people, as many other people's prayers have proved useful to me.

In *There's a Time and a Place*, the sections follow the Church calendar chronologically from Advent to All Saints; each section begins with a theme prayer for the season.

The first Index lists all the prayers in their printed order, together with titles. Since the prayers arise out of scriptural meditation, for each a keynote text is given, together with the sequence of main references and scriptural allusions. This may help someone using the book for private devotion to think my thoughts after me – and to better them, since he is going to the source; and it is possible that in some cases the sequence of allusive reference may yield the outline of a meditation or address to which the prayer would be a responsive summing up.

The index of Main Source References places in biblical order the passages from which the keynote texts are taken.

The remaining two indexes are primarily intended for the person preparing public worship.

Some prayers were originally used before or after a particular hymn, and a few will be significantly strengthened by such a juxtaposition; hence the index of Related Hymns.

The index, The Place of the Prayers in Worship attempts to place each prayer in one or more of five movements which are discernible in modern free church worship. The movements correspond often but not inflexibly to the sequence of items in a service: in worship as in any personal encounter, the 'approach' expressed at the first greeting retains its importance and may be reaffirmed at any point; so the credal element appropriate in the opening of a service reasserts itself later in word and sacrament. Similarly the movement of 'offering' may well overflow the 'offertory'; nor need 'family awareness' be confined to a children's address. Often a service finds its climax in an expression of commitment, but many would say that the concluding note should be one of thanksgiving or praise. These are the five movements as I see them:

1 *Approach*. The congregation *locates itself*, takes bearings on its own life, on God (relating itself to him *gratefully*, because he is good, and *penitently*, because we are not), and on its faith – which is later restated in sermon or sacrament or both.

2 *Family awareness*. Room is made in worship for the congregation to remind itself that it is a community with no
   upper or lower age limit.

3 *Offering*. This movement is aptly focused in the giving of
   money and of the Communion bread and wine.

4 *Intercession*. The congregation exercises 'the priesthood of
   all believers'.

5 *Commitment and petition*. Worship reaches a climax in the
   believer's renewed sense of his privileged standing in the
   sight of God, as redeemed by grace through faith. At this
   point, our self-consecration to God, and the urgent
   presentation to him of our deepest need, are perceived to
   be inseparable.

A last word about length. Many of these prayers take licence
from the nonconformist tradition of the 'long prayer', and are
long; *too* long for a collect, too long for use without careful
preparation. They contain internal rhythms, climaxes and
pauses, changes of tempo; a long prayer needs to be *performed*;
and why not? When we think of a cantor or a precentor it is
obvious that his leading of worship is one of the performing
arts: the performance as well as its content is offered to God.
It is perhaps too rarely realised that anyone who leads
worship is also a performer in precisely the same way, with
the same responsibility. Even when the prayers used are only
short ones.

JAMIE WALLACE

College Street Baptist Church, Northampton
October 1981

I believe in
God the Father Almighty, maker of heaven and earth,
and in Jesus Christ his only Son, our Lord . . .

Advent

1

'Our God is coming . . .'   Ps 50:3

You are the God who came,
                who comes,
                who is to come.

You came in Jesus
All that prepared the way for him was part of your coming:
        the promise to Abraham, poets' visions,
        prophets of judgment and hope.

You come in the Spirit
who makes Christ immediate,
        opening our eyes to see him
        in the neighbour who serves us
        and the neighbour we can serve.

You are to come
at the end of all time and the end of our time
        in the judgment of Christ and the mercy of Christ
        and the glory of Christ
        as he promised.

★

Bring us peace
in the knowledge that you have come
in Christ born, crucified and risen
so that, already,
    all is changed.

Keep us alert
to your coming day by day
in the truth we can learn, the good we can do,
the love we can share.
May our repentance, our obedience and our joy
    daily welcome you.

Make us wise
in the expectation of your coming at last
to judge the past and finish the future
    and resume eternity.

★

O come, O come, Immanuel.
Creator Spirit, come.
O day of God, draw near.

2

An Opening Prayer

'But when the right time finally came, God sent his own Son . . .'
Gal 4:4

God our heavenly Father:
in the fullness of time
you sent forth your Son
to be our Redeemer,
    leading us to everlasting life,
    and promising to all who believe
    deliverance from sin
    and mercy in that final judgment
    which, with your final victory,
    shall surely come to pass.

Now and at all times
tune our hearts to sing your praise
and our minds to hear your word,
through the same Jesus Christ our Lord.

3

From the Waiting Earth

'Salvation is to be found through him alone . . .' Acts 4:12

O promised Christ:
we are a world at war
and our peace depends on your coming.

We are a sinful people
and our pardon depends on your coming.

We are full of good intentions but bad at keeping promises;
our only hope of doing God's will
is that you should come and help us do it.

Lord Christ, Son of the Father, giver of the Spirit,
our world waits
for your peace,
for your pardon,
and for your grace.

Even so come, Lord Jesus.

4

From the waiting Church

'. . . to God be glory in the church and in Christ Jesus . . .'
Eph 3:21

Heavenly Father: you have given your Son to the world as
    its Saviour
and your Holy Spirit to the Church as her strength.
Then why is the world still so dark,
why is the Church still so weak?

★

We thank and honour you
for all that your gracious love has done:
the wars you have made to cease,
the sick you have healed,
and the saints whom you have made holy and strong.

We thank you for what you did in past years
to revive and unify your Church;
we glory still in the days
of which our fathers tell,
when faith raged like an epidemic
in Scottish islands and Welsh hills and English shires;
and before, when your Patrick made Ireland a green
    heaven.

★

But, God, it is *now*
that you have called us to live and serve,
it is now that we know our need of you;
if the miracles the world needs now are to be wrought,
we need you as though you had never come before.

As at the first,
make straight your way in our hearts.
Prepare the way of the Lord
in the routines of our worship and our habitual church life.
Stir up in us the spirit of penitence and prayer,
and a great hopefulness

as of those who watch by night,
knowing the dawn will come.

Set our minds on you;
may we seek to be about your business,
and look for your blessing on ours.
Hallow the comings and goings of friendship and
  neighbourhood.
Sting us into action
as the hearers of the first Baptist were stung,
so that we may be baptised in mind and in behaviour,
in affection and habit and purse.

Make your Church your people,
and make your people the instruments of your love.

So may our peace with you be the beginning
of the world's peace.
So may our hearts be again the Bethlehem where Christ is
  born,
for all the shepherds and kings of the world
to come and see.

5

Prayer of Suppressed Excitement

'. . . my soul is glad because of God my Saviour . . .'
Lk 1:46–55

God and Father of us all:
we thank you for this exciting time of year.
Parcels are wrapped and hidden, secrets are kept,
good things are cooked in the kitchen and stored in the
  freezer
ready for the Christmas feast.
It is the time of looking forward,
hastening the day, but spinning out the fun of preparation.
The eyes of parents and grandparents light up
with the glee they see in the children.

★

Lord, help the children
to hold and hallow the wonder that they feel,
this magic which is pure and undefiled because it is yours,
because it speaks the story of your love
in a coming to earth which happened once
and is always true.

Lord, keep us who are older aware of the wonder too;
quicken our senses if they have been dulled
with business and greed and comfort and worry
– and age;
so that we too may know again the desire, the impatience
and the joy
of Christmas.

God-with-us,
you have after all been longer with us than with the
     children,
had longer with us to show your abiding goodness.
We have had time to see more than the Babe in his manger:
we have knelt at the cross of the Crucified;
we have needed and we have felt
the healing touch of the Son of Man.
We have been guided to friends and to decisions,
to partners and places,
as surely as the wise men were guided
as they followed the Christmas star.
We have more, not less, than the children
to wonder at.

★

At Christmas we shall praise you
for the beginning of something which grew,
and has grown with us along the years.

Our soul doth magnify the Lord,
and our spirit hath rejoiced in God our Saviour;
for he that is mighty hath magnified us,
and worthy is his name,
which we know
in Jesus Christ.

6

Consecration

'Everything you do or say, then, should be done in the name of
the Lord Jesus, as you give thanks through him to God the Father.'
Col 3:17

Heavenly Father:
by your grace enable our celebration of Christmas
to be really a celebration of Christ.

As we look back in memory and in history,
seize us again with astonishment
at the fact
that Christ came.

As we look around us now,
in fear, in greed, and in friendliness,
may the awareness of Christ's presence transform our view
of all else.

And as we look forward,
in hope and apprehension, warn us and warm us
with the knowledge
that he who came into our past and comes into our present
must also be looked for in our future
on earth and in eternity.

In all our busy Christmassing may we be, as Jesus was,
about our Father's business,
which is nothing less
than the salvation of the world
and the transfiguration of all things
into heavenly glory.

So help us, heavenly Father,
for Jesus' sake.

7

On Jordan's Bank

'At that time John the Baptist came . . .'   Mt 3:1–13

O God:
before your beloved Son in whom you are well pleased
was made known to mankind in his baptism
and in his ministry,
you sent his herald John
with words of promise
and of warning.

As Christmas comes, and the memory of Christ's birth,
forgive us if we think so much of the wonderful promise
that we forget the sombre warning.

★

For our viperous generation also needs to repent
before it can believe the Gospel,
receive the Christ or enter the Kingdom.

We also love darkness rather than light
for our deeds also are evil;
we also look for man's praise before yours;
we also lay up for ourselves treasure upon earth
where our heart is.
We also set much store by our spiritual heritage,
forgetting that you can of these stones
raise up children
to Augustine and Cranmer,
to Bunyan and Helwys, to Carey,
to Wesley, Wilberforce, Booth, Clifford and Spurgeon,
even to . . . (*suitable local hero*).

★

Stern love of God, call us again to repentance,
so that we may be ready to rejoice in the comfort
of your mercy.
Open our eyes to the challenge of our day,
and our ears to what the Spirit says to the churches
now.

Call us once more to put first things first,
and first of them all your kingdom
and your righteousness.

Forgive our sins, renew our vision, deepen our love,
discipline our service;
so that your will may be done
in us as it is in heaven;
to the glory of your name,
in the power of your Spirit,
and by the grace of your Son Jesus Christ.

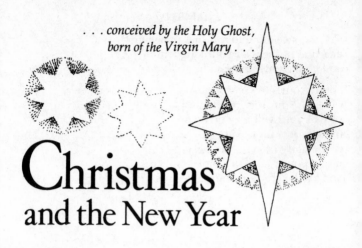

*. . . conceived by the Holy Ghost,
born of the Virgin Mary . . .*

Christmas
and the New Year

1

. . . the holy child will be called the Son of God.'
Lk 1:28, 30–33, 35

Marvel and mystery of Christmas:
that God should use human kind
not merely to serve his purpose
but to embody his being.

Father,
when in such great love you sent your son
to be the Word of life our ears could hear,
our eyes read and our fingers touch,
your Spirit lit frail flesh to make it so;
> took flesh of our flesh, bone of our bone,
> Christ's Mother, full of his grace.

We praise you
for this humbling of Godhead for our good,
the undeserved but indispensable stooping.
We honour you
> for the grace with which your Spirit
> filled our Lady.

And
we honour all mothering and all manhood born of woman
since they have been thus touched by your majesty
and honoured by your use;
    since Christ is born
    our Lord and Brother.

We worship you
and reverence all human life
for his sake.

2

Bidding Prayer for a Service of Lessons and Carols

'. . . she gave birth to her first son . . .'   Lk 2:4–7

This is a time to rejoice
    in the knowledge that Christ was born at Bethlehem,
    God's Son in David's city,
    God's Word of love made flesh for our redemption.
This is a time to remember
    the first Christmas
    and all the Christmasses we have known,
    with gratitude that so much joy has come into our lives
    through the Father's love,
    the Son's presence
    and the Spirit's power.
This is a time to remember one another
    in good fellowship and Christian love.
This is a time to remember the unfortunate,
    the sorrowful and the lonely.
This is a time to remember the world which God loves so
    much,
    in its need of peace,
    in its need of justice,
    in its need of the good news of Jesus.

Let us pray

Gracious God and heavenly Father:
we praise and glorify your name

for your great love shown at the first Christmas
in the birth of your Son our Saviour Jesus.

Be present in our happy remembrance of your mighty acts,
    as we listen to the story of mankind's redemption
        and sing the carols.

By your Holy Spirit come into our Christmas rejoicing
at church and at home;
forgive and correct our selfishness,
and help us celebrate Christmas
to the honour of Christ.

In his name we ask it,
and in his words we pray,
saying,
    Our Father. . . .

3

Silent Night

'The Lord is in his holy Temple; let everyone on earth be silent
                    in his presence.'   Hab 2:20

God gave the hallelujah angels their head
and shepherds overheard the joyful noise,
but the rest was silence,
or almost silence.

The shuffling of sleepy beasts in stable straw,
the creak of a swinging door,
soft urgent words from an anxious husband,
small sounds of a nursing mother and her child.

Silently a seed begins to be a great tree;
silently God and a few men ponder the transformation
of the world's destiny.

A guilty king was right to fear for his throne
but the threat he dreaded
didn't even cry.

Blessed be God for silence:
silence of understanding between friends,
silence of devotion,
silence of peace.

Blessed be God for the silence
of a bitter word unspoken,
a kindly thought kept secret.

Blessed be God for the quiet coming
of the King of kings;
lest children be frightened,
lest it be thought he comes in pride or vengeance,
lest we should fall into the error
of confusing loudness with truth.

Blessed be God for the silence of light shining in darkness
and love made known in humility
through Jesus Christ our Lord.

4

In the Quiet of Christmas Eve and the Darkness of a Stable

'. . . Mary, who sat down . . . and listened . . .'
Lk 10:39, 42

Lord Jesus,
you once praised Mary of Bethany for being the quiet one
sitting and waiting for you to speak
instead of bustling around like her sister Martha
who was so kind, but so bothered and anxious.

★

It was quiet in the stable that night in Bethlehem,
after the strain of travelling
and the scrimmage in the streets of the crowded little town
at census time.

Nothing to do, for that other Mary, your Mother,
but to sit and wait for your coming
and, when you had come, to sit quietly and watch
by the manger where you lay.

★

Here we are now
in the quietness of this Christmas Eve.
Some of us are tired out with shopping and cooking
and decorating,
and we need a rest.
Some of us are very young and sleepy already;
bed time soon, and we shall be fast asleep
so that Santa Claus can come,
and so that we can be bright and happy tomorrow.
Some of us are really a bit old now for the Christmas rush,
too old for the great scramble to do what Christmas entails:
we'd sooner sit quietly and think about what Christmas
    means.

★

So in imagination we sit or kneel in the hushed stable,
the cave cut in the rock, with straw on the floor
and animals dozing nearby.
The flicker of a lantern here indoors, and the stars outside,
are all the light there is –
except that among the stars, one star shines brighter for
    Jesus;
and in the manger is Jesus himself,
the Light of the world.

★

Lord Jesus, give us your peace,
and in the peace may we see your light –
peace to live in and light to walk in.

★

Lord Jesus,
we welcome you into our world,

into human life,
into our hearts.
Thank you for coming
to teach and heal, to befriend and lead,
and to die for our salvation.
Thank you for being here now
as you promised you would be
whenever we gather
in your name.

5

On Christmas Eve
a Prayer of Thanksgiving and Defiance

'The Light shines in the darkness . . .'   Jn 1:5

Lord Jesus Christ,
Son of God and baby in Bethlehem:
we thank you for coming
to be the Light of our world.

Help us by your Holy Spirit
to catch and echo
the song of the angels –
'Glory to God in the highest!'

Give us the impudence to sing with them
of peace on earth and goodwill among men.
Give us the defiant joy
which will not be sober in this high festival.

Hear, we pray – and make us hear – the cry
of our brothers and sisters in pain
and under oppression:
busy us with errands of mercy and love.

But never let the light of joy be dimmed
or the shouts of glee subdued
on Jesus' birthnight –
Let day's children defy the dark with your glory.

For Christ is born, though the bomb drop tomorrow,
Christ is born, though this be the *last* Nowell;
Christ is born to say God loves the world
and joy shall win.

Yet even as we shout, daring the devil with Christian
    merriment,
and celebrate the best of births,
may your grace grant, at the still centre where the soul is,
silence

and make us, Lord, as those who wait
like Mary and Joseph with obedience
for the wonder of what you will do *for* us
and the discipline of what you will do *in* us.

6

Upon the Midnight Clear
– a Prayer after 'Two Thousand Years of Wrong' . . .

'. . . the world did not recognise him. . . . Some . . . did receive him. . . .'
Jn 1:10–12

Forgive us, Lord God,
that we and our fathers
and our fathers' fathers
for untold generations
have so little heeded
the love song that the angels sing.

Prophets had come
helping your law to highlight
the sin and folly of mankind;
and they had promised
that your love would come
to change all, and set all to rights.

Your Love came,
but there was no room
in tavern or heart for him to enter

and be born decently
with a proper welcome
from those he came to heal.

Small wonder that the wrong went on
from year to year:
war and pain and man-made wretchedness.
What else did we deserve but darkness
when we would not have the Light?
But the Light was not to be put out.

Your Love was undiscouraged,
killed but alive again and unkillable;
and there was welcome for him
in some hearts –
even in some taverns
some paid heed.

Forgive us, Lord God,
for all our sins and stupidity, ours
and those of generations past, past telling.
Receive our praise and thanks
that some have heeded
and made us hear.

7

Responsive Prayer for Christmas Morning

'. . . singing praises to God . . .'   Lk 2:8–17

God our Father: you so loved the world
that you gave your only begotten Son
so that whoever believed in him might not perish
but have everlasting life.
When we think of this
  we want to shout and sing for joy.

Those who sought him in a palace were mistaken
and had to be redirected to a stable.

Humble shepherds arrived there first and were less
    surprised:
God's angel had told them what to expect
– a peasant baby, swaddled and laid in the straw of a
    manger,
for the Son of God was born to simple folk.
When we think of this
    we want to shout and sing for joy.

He came not to be waited on, but to serve other people.
He healed the sick and taught the ignorant.
He made friends with people whom polite society
had given up for lost.
He came to save people from their sins.
When we think of this
    we want to shout and sing for joy.

He came to live a life which ended terribly:
disgrace, betrayal, death, even the death of the cross.
The way we treated him makes us sorry and ashamed;
but his death shows more than anything else
the lengths your love will go to for our sake.
When we think of this
    we want to shout and sing for joy.

What began in a stable did not end with the cross.
When you raised him from the dead,
the Bethlehem Baby who became the Man of Sorrows
proved himself the Lord of Life.
And what began with twelve friends
has become a worldwide family, and a fellowship
which extends from earth to heaven.
Thanks to Jesus,
as we praise you this morning we are, quite literally,
part of the heavenly host.
When we think of this
    we want to shout and sing for joy.

8

Prayer by Those who are Merry, for Those who Probably Aren't

'Be happy with those who are happy, weep with those who weep.'
Rom 12:15

Lord God:
here amid the decorations on your Son's birthday,
we remember people who, like Mary and Joseph in
      Bethlehem,
have nowhere nice to live,
or nowhere to live at all:
homeless through natural disaster
or man's mistakes and misdeeds.
We pray for Christian Aid, Shelter   *(others can be added or
      substituted)*
and all the people and organisations
that try to help.

We remember those who are ill, at home or in hospital,
especially . . . . ,
and the people who are taking care of them.

We remember all who have sad thoughts today despite the
      festival
because they are away from home,
or because loved ones have gone from them.
Give them today happy memories,
some good friends,
and the certainty of homecoming and reunion
in this world or the next.

We pray for all who go in fear of violence even on
      Christmas Day,
and for those whose business it is to try and reassure them:
armed forces, policemen and good neighbours,
and the world's peace-makers.

We pray for everyone today suffering remorse for past sins,
and admit before you the things which trouble our own
      conscience;

we pray for all who by their faith and your grace are able
to speak your word of forgiveness and hope,
and preach the good news of Jesus Christ

who teaches us to pray:

Our Father. . . .

NEW YEAR

9

At the Gate of the Year

'. . . I, the Lord your God, am with you wherever you go.'

Josh 1:1–9

Who dares venture into a new day, let alone a new year,
without the assurance of greater help
than man can give?
So it is, Lord God
that we turn to you.

★

We do not turn to you as though we had any rightful claim
upon your help,
but as sinners who have constantly let you down.
We have not lived up to our own aspirations,
and still less to your commands.
We have sinned, we have despaired, we have idled;
we have been lacking in compassion
and the finer points
of friendship and love.
Too often charity has not even begun at home,
and when it has, it has stayed there.
Our love is narrow and our hopes are low,
and our actions prove it, again and again.
But you have been faithful, keeping all your promises to us;
your mercy flows freely in forgiveness and grace.
You have even enabled us to serve you

and in that service you have blessed us
with encouragement.

★

So we turn to you
as men and women repentant, needy and grateful,
who find strength, joy and peace
in the knowledge of your love
and the fact of your grace.

★

We thank you that New Year follows so closely upon
        Christmas;
so that when we most sense and fear the future
our mind and spirit have just been fortified
with the glad tidings of great joy
to all people, for all time:
        that to us has been born a Saviour who is Christ the
        Lord,
        Lord of history, Redeemer of mankind,
        Conqueror of devils and death,
        Good Shepherd and slain Lamb
        who takes away the sin of the world.

★

Whatever we must go without
of certainty or courage
as we step into 19 ,
grant us to know the love of Christ,
and to be strengthened with might
by his Spirit in the inner man.
For his sake
and in his name
we ask it.

10

God with Us, Go with Us

'. . . so high are my ways and thoughts above yours.'

Is 55:8–9

Heavenly Father:
your ways are higher than our ways
and your thoughts longer than our thoughts.
You are from everlasting to everlasting
and a thousand ages in your sight
are like an evening gone.

Yet you have in love reached down
to touch our little time
with your eternity,
and our life
with life everlasting
in Christ.

Go with us now
into the future you have in mind for us.
Cast out our fear;
fill us with faith
and hope
and love;
through the grace
of Jesus, your Son, our Saviour.

Epiphany

1

'. . . If one of you wants to be great . . .' Mk 10: 42–45

O Christ,
dawn star of the new day:
to the brightness of your rising
kings came.

If the King of kings could be born in a stable,
there recognized
and honoured,
all authority had henceforth to be seen
in a new light.

What an awesome thing it is
to bear authority,
now that the Lord
has been patronised by a scholar,
    hailed as a kindred spirit by an NCO
    and sentenced by a provincial judge.

Glorious Lord,
govern all our ruling,

whether we have charge of a nation or a church,
      a union, a business or a family,
         or just a day that we can call our own.

Keep us reminded
that all authority is given from above
and that those who hold it for a time
do not have
the glory,
which is yours alone.

2

New Light

'. . . He will cause the bright dawn . . . to shine from
heaven on all those who live in the dark shadow . . .'
                                                    Lk 1:78–9

Lord Jesus Christ:
when you were born
a new light shone
into the life of mankind.
Shepherds ran to see
in a humble cowshed
the truth of the gleaming angel's message.
Kings came
to the brightness of your rising.
The glory of the Lord was revealed
and all sorts of people
saw it together.

★

Lord Jesus Christ,
bright and morning star,
dayspring from on high:
shine for us.

★

In the light of your goodness
may we see our sins

and repent of them
and be forgiven.
In the light of your love
may we see the purpose
which you have for our lives
and live them to your glory.

★

For your name's sake.

3

The Journey of the Magi, and Others

'. . . men who studied the stars came from the east . . .'
Mt 2:1

Shepherds hurried from nearby hills when your Son was
   born,
wise men travelled from the east
following a star.
O God we pray
for all who make journeys,
asking that all human travelling
may lead men and women nearer to you.

★

We remember those who, at Christmas time,
drive to parties.
May they have safe going and a good welcome;
may they carry with them love and joy
as their most important gifts;
and may no party spirit spoil by accident
the journey home.

★

We pray for those who travel in haste
to bring help where things have gone wrong:
those whose journey is by fire engine, ambulance or police
   car,

lifeboat or rescue helicopter.
Give to those whose journeys are duty
while other people make holiday,
the joy of service and the value added
of being needed.

★

We pray for those travelling
through sorrow, doubt and illness,
especially when the journey seems long
and not very hopeful.
Bless them with the blessing of the wise men
who travelled far, by starlight only,
yet at the end of the way found glory.

★

We pray for those whose way lies in the darkness
of hatred and spite,
and who go on journeys
to hurt, frighten and destroy.
May the light of Christmas in their hearts
show a better way of improving the world
than by spoiling it.
Forgive them,
and forgive us all,
for the sins which wreck the world you love
and grieve your Spirit.

★

We ask it in his name
who is the journey's end
that wise men seek,
Jesus Christ our Lord.

4

Gifts for the King

'. . . their gifts of gold, frankincense, and myrrh . . .'

Mt 2:11

King Jesus,
we bring you our gold:
> talents your Father gave us,
> skills we have acquired,
> a little money, a little power,
> a little success perhaps
> and plenty of ambition.

These we offer to you
so that you may make them really worth something
in your kingdom.

Jesus, great High Priest,
we bring you our frankincense:
> deep needs and longings
> which are sometimes easier to admit in church:
> the need for forgiveness and peace,
> the need for friendship and love to get and to give;
> the wish to do good and the knowledge
> that we must have help if we are to do it.

Lord help us,
pray for us.

Jesus, crucified Saviour,
we bring you our myrrh:
> shadows on our path,
> weakness, illness, limitations,
> grief for ourselves and others,
> our knowledge of parting and pain.

These we offer to you
so that what we bear may be touched with the holiness
of what you bore for us;
and so that by your grace we may have part
in the world's redemption.

5

'At his Appearing'

'. . . to bring us the knowledge of God's glory . . .' 2 Cor 4:6

Lord God, they marvelled at your Son's appearing.

> Shepherds had been told of him by angels
> and when they hurried to see,
> it was all as wonderful
> as the angel voice had said.
> Wise men had learned of the new-born King
> from the rising of a star
> and from their science and statecraft;
> they too came obediently
> and found a Child worthy of worship.
> Old Simeon and saintly Anna had listened
> to what the prophets said,
> had yearned and prayed for Messiah's birth;
> one day a Child was brought for blessing
> to the Temple,
> brought by country parents
> in town for the census.
> Anna and Simeon saw him for what he is:
> the Lord of heaven
> born on the earth
> for our salvation.

Lord God: we thank you for what we have seen of your
glory
in the face of Jesus Christ.

> We have seen
> the faces of children around a Christmas crib.
> We have seen
> the joy of the converted at their baptism.
> Christ has appeared to us
> in people visibly transformed
> because he has touched them
> with his grace.
> At our conversion, and each turning of the way

when we have stepped out in faith,
he has shone for us – one way or another –
like a guiding star.
In patient, undramatic, private ways he has told us,
'I am with you; do not be afraid.'
He has appeared to us.

With shepherds and kings, with the aged and the very
        young,
with the wise and simple of every century who have seen
        the Lord
with eye of flesh or eye of faith,
we lift up our hearts in praise,
and welcome again the Child born to be King
– a King who lived our childhood and died our death.
Lord God: in his name
we give you glory.

6

*On the Twelfth Day of Christmas
a Responsive Prayer*

'. . . I say it again: rejoice!'   Phil 4:4–8

O God, your love came down at Christmas.
*This we believe
    and in this we will rejoice.*

In a world where much is wrong,
nevertheless your grace is at work
and your Spirit moves.
*This we believe
    and in this we will rejoice.*

Despite the things which frighten and hurt,
people are kind, generous and brave
because your light shines for them
and in them.
*This we believe
    and in this we will rejoice.*

You ask us to help the world in its sorrow,
but not to let its sorrow take away our joy,
because joy is your gift
and must be cherished.
This we believe
  and in this we will rejoice.

Since Christ is in the world
and in our hearts
there is hope.
So there should be merriment
in our hearts
and in our homes.
This we believe
  and in this we will rejoice.

Christ is born,
born for us,
the King and Saviour of mankind.
This we believe
  and in this we will rejoice.

. . . was crucified . . .

Lent

1

> '. . . God was making all mankind his friends through
> Christ . . . and he has given us the message . . .'
> 2 Cor 5:18–19

Immortal, invisible God:
you show yourself to us in Jesus who was crucified.

What we know of you is what we see in him,
and we see him –
  tired
  famished
  saddened
  betrayed
  despised
  forsaken.

Like his apostle after him he died daily;
his crucifixion began before Calvary.

In Christ we see you
accepting from your creation not only its praise
but its rejection, its defiance, its scorn,
its simply not noticing you.

In Christ you were reconciling the world to yourself
    as a father shows himself obstinately at one with his
      children
    who give him love, and much else, and much worse,
    and whom he still loves.

Father, by your Son's grace enable us
to accept your world and your other children
entire,
as he did.

In the power of his cross may we take up ours
and, reconciled, be reconcilers too,
in his name.

2

Implications

'. . . believe also in me.'   Jn 14:1

Lord Jesus Christ:
we believe in you and in the heavenly father who sends
    you.
We believe that you and he are one
with the Holy Spirit who makes you known to us.
We praise and love in you what is highest and best
in our experience and beyond it.
In loving you we set our hearts
on that which will not change, diminish or turn against us.

★

Our hearts should not then be troubled, Lord.

★

Forgive and increase our little faith;
replenish our supply of grace;
give us your peace.
Graft our lives into your life,

so that as branches of the one true Vine
we may bear much spiritual fruit
to the glory of God.

★

Now as we take your words and speak them in prayer
grant us more than your words to speak with:
may we live with your life,
act with your power,
love with your love,
and go on growing into your likeness
who could first and rightly say,
'Our Father. . . .'

3

For all Seasons

'. . . when the Son of Man came, he ate and drank . . .'
Mt 11:16–19

Lord Jesus:
you liked going to parties
and were also prepared to spend forty hungry days in the
    desert.
Help us to accept whole-heartedly
both the pleasures and the disciplines of life
to the glory of your heavenly Father.

4

Profitable Exchange

'. . . whoever loses his life for me . . .'   Mk 8:35 etc.

Jesus,
you gave yourself for us.
Help us to give ourselves to you;
so that we may get ourselves back

in the miracle of your friendship
which is for ever.
For you are the King
and you keep your promises.

5

Love Limited, for Love's Sake

'. . . of his own free will, he gave up all he had . . .'

Phil 2:7

Lord Jesus Christ:
in great humility you have come where we are.
Prince of heaven,
you accepted the limits and frustrations of human life
in a world spoilt by human sin.

Why, Lord?
You love us so much?
You want us set free to live
    in the light
    and the truth
    and the freedom
    of your Father's house?

Thank you, Lord.
We call you Master and Lord
and so you are.
Help us to receive your truth,
    to follow your example,
    and to take your way – the way of the cross
    which leads to glory.

6

The Lord is my Light

'Whoever follows me . . . will never walk in darkness.'

Jn 8:12

Lord Jesus Christ:
we thank you for your call to each one of us
to be your disciple and servant.
Help us to see,
in the light of your wonderful love,
what we are.

And tell us *where* we are,
by your voice in the people around us
and in the hints supplied by circumstance.

Grant us a vision of your purpose
in ordinary things,
and a sense of the value you place
on what we do
in our everyday work,
in church life,
in home duties,
and in facing the reality of sorrow and conflict.

If you are challenging us to the heroism of staying put,
give us the grace we need for constancy;
if you are calling us to get up and go, to change our place
or improve our performance,
then give us the grace we need for that.

And, Lord,
if despite our prayer and readiness
the vision is not yet clear,
and if the call
is still to days of drabness
with little seeming value or importance,
give us the grace of patience and a quiet cheerfulness.
Store up for us a future realisation
that all was not in vain,
and that every step of the way
you were leading.

7

Prayers for a Bible Study Series on the First Letter of Peter

I

'. . . this is the true grace . . . Stand firm in it.' 1 Peter 5:12

Grace reached down
speaking a Word made flesh to save the world.

Grace reaches out:
across the years I hear the Crucified
forgive me for betraying him.

Grace reaches forward:
the Spirit in us craves and pledges
a day of judgment, mercy and remaking,
to crown with glory him who deserves it
and us who do not.

★

God, in your grace which sought and found me,
hold me fast.

II

'. . . you love him, although you have not seen him . . .' 1 Peter 1:8

Seeing Jesus
is something I am denied
and also spared.

★

There was no instant magic in his physical presence
to compel belief or make the foolish wise.
When silly things were said atop the shining mountain
or rash feet sank in deep waters of failing faith,
embarrassment was immediate;
and at cockcrow, when one's eyes met his – what shame.
No, I have lost my childhood envy of the Galileans.

★

Saviour, forgive and grow my little love
till it can bear to look on you.

III

'. . . the chosen race, the King's priests, God's own people . . .'
1 Peter 2:9

Born again!
Not only to lightened conscience and the hope of heaven
but to a belonging and a heritage –
all we ever envied Jews is ours, and their trials,
in Christ of crown and cross.

★

Born again to royalty and priesthood!
Not the status merely but the task:
kings have no private life, priests little leisure;
rule, worship, intercession tell on mind and body –
the idle saved had best beware God's revolution.

★

So help us, Lord, to *do* what you intended
when you caused us to be reborn.

IV

'. . . submit . . .' 1 Peter 2:13, 5:5 etc

We need brave gifts – give them, victorious Christ –
to stand against the devil and do good.
Yet this is the hardest virtue
to have or understand or ask:
> this meek silence by which a prisoner judges
> the law and the derision he submits to;
> this mastery a Master shows
> with basin and towel for disciples' feet;
> this love in which obedience and consideration meet
> to make not one slavery but two freedoms.
For this your *gifts* are not enough.
Your *nature* must be in us. Come, Lord, come.

V

'My dear friends, do not be surprised . . .' 1 Peter 4:12

Life in God's love
is new every morning – and new every Christian.
Which is why we are all surprised
when it turns out so eventful.

★

We have been warned:
all things ours in Christ, with persecutions.
Forgive us, Lord,
if we are oftener astonished than we should be.

★

Make us so expectant of blessing
and so armed against attack,
that neither may surprise us
and both may bring you glory.

Mothering Sunday
and Other Family Occasions

1

About Family Life
– what we believe, what we confess, what we need

'. . . on my knees before the Father . . .' Eph 3:14–15

God our heavenly Father
from whom every family in heaven and on earth takes its
      name:
you set a standard for human parents,
a glory of which we all fall short.
    No earthly father loves like you,
    no mother half so mild
    bears and forbears as you have done. . . .

God the Son our Saviour
obeying your Father in heaven,
loving your brothers and sisters on earth:
you were obedient unto the death of the cross,
you loved to the uttermost.
    We sons and daughters of God and man,
    wayward and prodigal,

stand sinful in the light of your pure countenance.
Only your grace can make us
into obedient children of God
and loving children of men – and it must happen or we
    die.

God the Holy Spirit,
filling, uniting and expressing the Godhead,
bringing order into creation and fellowship into the Church:
you set a standard for all our family feeling.
    Our coldness, rancour and feuding,
    and all the nastiness for which
    we blame the generation gap,
    merits your judgment
    and needs your breath of life and love.

Father, we have sinned and are no more worthy to be called
your children; bless us, Father, for we have sinned.
Jesus, Son of David, have mercy on us in our darkness
and paralysis of soul; say to us,
'Son, daughter, sister, brother, your sins are forgiven',
and restore to us the right to be God's children.
Come, *Holy Spirit* to cleanse and renew us
and keep us in the knowledge and love of God;
give us the mind of Christ.
Unite our families in the heavenly family,
by the power of the heavenly Father and his love,
by the grace of Jesus Christ and his sacrifice
    unto the praise and glory
    of the One God, Father, Son and Holy Spirit.

2

A Litany of Family Thanksgiving

'Then the Lord God said, "It is not good for the man to live alone . . ."'
                                       Gen 2:18

Creator God and loving Father:
You knew it was not good for man to be alone.
You have made us dependent on one another.

You have set us in families.
In our need of company
　　We thank you for one another

Loving Father:
You have given us hearts able and wanting to overflow in
　　　　love
to neighbour and friend, to lover, partner and child,
to those we pity, those we admire
and those we delight in.
In our need to love
　　We thank you for one another

You send us into the world not self-supporting
but dependent.
We have to depend on forbears for our roots, parents for
　　　　our homes.
As we must give to one another in love, so we must take,
life-long, from those who go before us.
In our need of nurture
　　We thank you for one another

Sorrow can be borne if there is sympathy;
joy is not fully joyous unless we can celebrate together;
achievement is complete only when we have been
　　　　congratulated;
good fortune turns rancid
if we keep it to ourselves.
In our need to share
　　We thank you for one another

When we are young, you give us elders who love us
for what we are not yet;
midway, you bless us with brothers, sisters and cousins
who may like us for what we are;
when we are old, you sometimes allow us, in your grace,
a few progeny to honour us
for what we have been.
In our need of esteem
　　We thank you for one another

At the right moment there is nothing so unforgettable

as the prayer learned from a mother;
nothing so arresting as a father's rebuke;
nor so persuasive
as a brother's witness.
In our need to hear your Word
We thank you for one another

The household of faith is stronger
than one believing heart.
In our need of Christian fellowship
We thank you for one another

Father in heaven,
from whom every family on earth takes something,
since we are made in your likeness:
receive our thanksgiving
for our childhood, our parenthood,
our roots and our *belonging*,
in Jesus Christ your Son
and our Brother.

3

A Litany of Family Concern

'For the sake of my relatives and friends . . .'   Ps 22:8

O God, Father of men and giver of good:
we bring to you the families of your people
in their *joy*.
 Where parents are loving
 and children are lively,
 where home is comfortable
 and jobs are secure,
 may our joy be hallowed by thanksgiving
 and our happiness increased by the sharing of it.
Father, amid the blessings you send
 keep us mindful of you who send them.

Son of God, Saviour of men,
joy and sword for Mary's heart:

we bring to you the families of your people
in their *sorrow*.
> Where grief has come
> for a loved one, or the love, that is no more;
> where jobs or home are lost
> or health has failed;
> where neighbours or relatives make trouble
> and children are wayward;
> where one or another is left coping
> with more than they bargained for
> and nobody laughs or sings,

Lord Jesus, in our desert and our Gethsemane
give us your grace of strength and peace.

Holy Spirit of unity, wisdom and love:
we bring to you the families of your people
in their *growth*.
> Reconcile us with the fact of change
> in one another, and in ourselves.
> Teach us that love need not be unaltering
> in order to be constant.
> Show us the loveliness
>> of the baby face
>> grown pimply with puberty;
>> the beauty of strong hands
>> grown waxen-veined in age.
> Strengthen our relationships
>> by contradiction and temper
>> as well as by acquiescence and peace.

Creator Spirit, keep us all growing up
till heaven dawns, to stretch us further still.

Father, Son and Spirit; providence, grace and love:
fit our families for the life of the heavenly household,
and for the service of mankind.
O Lord our God, make your way in our hearts
and be glorified in the manner of our life together.

. . . was . . . dead and buried . . .

Passiontide

1

'This is what is written: the Messiah must suffer . . .'
Lk 24:45–48

From the day of palms
through days of dispute
to the evening of fellowship, established and betrayed,
to the afternoon of the cross
and the night of death. . . .

God, we are ashamed. You came so close
and we did not know:
only looking back we can see.

You needed our hosannas, and we shouted them.
That at least we did.
You needed our love, and in the ointment and at table we
gave it;
but then, wearying, we slept; frightened, we ran;
challenged, we denied.

You were alone.
'My people, my people, why have you forsaken me?'

was what you did not say.
You reproached not us but your Father.
We were not there.
It was between you and him
in the Spirit whose groanings cannot be uttered
– a private anguish
    as parents break their hearts
    over an uncomprehending child.

Still we do not understand, but this we know:
your anguish is the saving of us.

Saviour, Spirit, Father God:
in hushed tears
we thank you.

2

The King Comes to our City

'. . . and when he saw it, he wept over it . . .' Lk 19:41–42

Almighty God:
we remember before you
the days in which your Son our Saviour
set his face steadfastly to go up to Jerusalem.
He was coming to his own
and his own were not going to receive him.
In the day of salvation
the city of David would not know
the things which belonged to her peace.

★

Heavenly Father:
as we look forward to Easter,
make in our minds a Jerusalem
to which Jesus may once more come.
By your grace make us able, in Spirit and in truth,
to shout Hosanna for the King
and sing Hallelujah at his rising,

without meantime crucifying him afresh
through our sinful hardness of heart.

★

We ask this for his name's sake.

3

Responsive Prayer for Palm Sunday

'. . . so I will give him a place of honour . . .' Is 53:10–12

Minister: *O Christ who once rode humbly into Jerusalem*
Everyone: *We salute you in your heavenly majesty.*

Lord Jesus, yours was a bitter journey,
a road that led from the cries of 'Hosanna'
to the shrieks of 'Crucify him'.
And we believe it was for us. . . .
O Christ who once rode humbly into Jerusalem
we salute you in your heavenly majesty.

Your whole life was a preparation for the way of the cross.
From high heaven you came all the way down
to little Bethlehem for your birth.
From Bethlehem where you had been welcomed and
worshipped
you and your Mother and Joseph fled as refugees to Egypt.
From Jerusalem where scholars had marvelled at your
boyish answers
you returned to Nazareth in subjection to your parents.
From baptism and anointing you were driven into the
desert
to be tempted by the devil.
From the mountain of transfiguration you came down again
to the valley where your disciples had failed.
Humiliation all the way
and all the way for us. . . .
O Christ who once rode humbly into Jerusalem
we salute you in your heavenly majesty.

After the humiliation came the glory.
You who so completely set aside all dignity
have been given the highest honour:
Head over all things to the Church,
throned in splendour,
to come again in power with all your angels.
Meanwhile and always you remember us,
interceding for us
at your Father's throne.
Your exaltation,
like your humbling
is for us. . . .
O Christ who once rode humbly into Jerusalem
  we salute you in your heavenly majesty.

Saviour we thank you
that on the first Palm Sunday
you rode as the King who comes in peace,
but unmistakably as the *king.*
So that for those who followed your royal progress that day
and for those who follow it still,
your royalty is unforgettable.
Even while, in faith and hope, we must wait
for your coronation
at the end of time. . . .
O Christ who once rode humbly into Jerusalem
  we salute you in your heavenly majesty.

4

Palm Sunday Petitions

'. . . Son of David, take pity on me!' Mk 10:47–48, cf. 11:10

Palm Sunday.
In the sunshine a holiday crowd
excited, their hope fed by rumours of miracles
– a man had been raised from death, some said.
Hope raised to certainty by hysteria
as excitement rose with the temperature.

Disciples surprised
at the extent of the crowd's enthusiasm for Jesus,
surprised at the Master's calm acceptance of homage.

And afterwards, now *long* afterwards,
after years of faith and worship, the deep conviction
that the royalty paraded before that Palm Sunday crowd
is the Majesty ruling the universe.

★

King Jesus: teach us that crowd's enthusiasm for you.
    Guard us from the dozing propriety
    of habitually religious people.
    Keep us convinced that you are terrific.
King Jesus: teach us your grace.
    You knew the crowd's fickleness,
    how deep their devotion went
    and how deep it didn't go.
    Graciously you accepted the tribute offered,
    knowing and forgiving its imperfection.
King Jesus: teach us your calm.
    You knew it was only for a day,
    the triumph and seeming success.
    A short week away there lay in wait for you
    betrayal, shame, agony, death.
    Yet you could live as you taught others to live,
    a day at a time,
    today's good unspoilt by tomorrow's evil.
King Jesus: teach us your power,
    which is your Father's power
    – to heal and reconcile,
      to give light and life,
      to endure and to win.
    Palm Sunday was too soon for triumph,
    but after desolation and dying
    triumph was coming.

Hosanna, King Jesus!
Hallelujah!

5

Palm Sunday
Offertory Prayer at a Family Service

'. . . one who humbles himself and becomes like this child . . .'
Mt 18:1–4

'The people of the Hebrews
With palms before Thee went.
Our praise and prayer and anthems
Before Thee we present.'

They shouted Hosanna – God save the King!
But instead of crowning you, Lord Jesus,
by the end of the week they had killed you.

Help us to mean it when we call you King,
help us to put you first, in the way we use
our time, our strength and our money.

Bless the gift we bring you now,
and make it work for your kingdom.
In your name we ask it.

6

Palm Sunday
An Opening Prayer at Evening Service

'. . . then Jesus went into the Temple . . .' Lk 19:29–46

Lord Jesus Christ:
it is Palm Sunday evening.
In the morning they cut palm branches,
waved them and shouted, 'Hosanna',
spread garments in the road for you to ride over,
hailed you Son of David
and King in Jerusalem – 'God save King Jesus!
Bless him for coming in the Lord's name!'
How your heart must have lifted.
This once at least they acclaimed you as King

and paid homage.
It must have given you strength
for the way of sorrow lying ahead.

★

But the sorrow began all too soon.
You saw the city in its holiday thoughtlessness cheering,
or plotting your death;
as ready to shout 'Crucify' as 'Hosanna',
ready to sell you for crucifixion
if the money was right
– and the leaders of God's people
doing the devil's work.
You wept.

★

In the Temple,
house of prayer for all peoples,
you found animals for sacrifice for sale,
blemished but still offered at inflated prices;
and money-changers making a fast shekel
out of tourists and pilgrims.

★

Through the morning
you basked, as might the Son of Man,
in the hosannas of the crowd.
In the evening
you wept and raged as might the Son of God,
to see his Father scorned
and his nation lost.

★

Christ our King,
as you rode into Jerusalem to the roar of the crowd
and the cheers of children,
so come into our excitement as we look forward to Easter.
But, of your grace,
enable us not to grieve you.

We ask it by your love
and for your Father's glory.

7

Suffering

'. . . we have a share in Christ's many sufferings . . .'
2 Cor 1:3–7

O God we commend to your blessing
all who suffer in mind or body according to the pattern
of Christ's greater pain.
We pray for those who feel themselves forsaken or
   betrayed,
and for people who, having worked and struggled,
have nothing to show for it except the signs and penalties
of failure.
We pray for the victims of injustice,
for all who must endure the scorn and mockery of lesser
   men,
and for those whose friends have all gone.
We pray for any who face a martyr's death.
We remember all who weep, and all who thirst.

★

Make it true for them
that the suffering of Christ has transfigured all suffering,
that the death of Christ has transfigured all death;
and that the victory of Christ
can be everyone's victory
through his grace.

8

Helping

'. . . Don't cry for me, but for yourselves . . .' Lk 23:26–31

O God, it is time to remember your Son's passion.
Remembering it, we pray for all who try to help
and find, as he did, that help is hard to give.

★

When we feel that other people's pride, their stupidity,
their greed, their anger, their silence or their chatter
prevent us from helping them,
help us to say, 'God knows', and know that it is true
– for he knows us, and *we* are hard for him to help.

★

For this also Christ suffered, suffered it at our hands,
he who came in love, and was destroyed
by us whom he came to save.

★

God grant us Christ's peace;
God teach us his patience;
for his sake.

9

Contrition and Hope

'. . . Surely, Lord, you don't mean me?' . . .   Mt 26:14–25

Judas betrayed you, Jesus his Master;
so did they all, each in his own way.

★

In the shadow of the cross
    we bring before you
        our own sense of shortcoming and failure,
        our share of the treachery.

For in the light of the cross
    we can bear to contemplate
    our lack of love,
    our weak faith and our failure of nerve,
    our deadly negligence in the doing of good.

We have denied, not you perhaps,
    but someone
    whom our good opinions would have helped.
We have betrayed, not you perhaps,
    but someone
    who had trusted us
    not to laugh behind his back.
We have rejected, not you perhaps,
    but someone
    who did not ask for much love or honour,
    but received from us none.

Here at the cross
    we traitors can bear,
    can just bear, the thought of our sin,
    because on the cross you said,
    'Father, forgive them.'
We can bear the thought
    because after you had risen from the tomb
    you sought out the very friends who had let you down
    and said, 'Fear not; be of good courage.'
    You said to Mary, 'The situation is changed,
    but not my love.'
    You said to Peter, 'Here is your commission renewed.'

★

Lord, grant us always to know
that even when we have despaired of ourselves,
you have not despaired of us.

GOOD FRIDAY

10

A Responsive Prayer for Good Friday
– 'His Grief and Ours'

'. . . he wept over it. . . . "Don't cry for me, but for yourselves." . . .'
Lk 19:41, 23:28

Lord Jesus: You looked at Jerusalem,
    God's city that had killed God's prophets
    and soon would crucify God's Son.
    You wept, not for yourself but for the sinful town
    which knew not the things that belonged to its peace.
    Our towns too, *this* town (city, village),
    are places you long to redeem and rule
    but, like the citizens of Jerusalem,
    we do not seem to know we need you.
Saviour, we remember your grief
    and we also grieve.

Lord Jesus: You looked at people.
    You knew what was in man
    yet you loved men and women,
    called them into your friendship and service.
    On the night of betrayal and shame
    they all forsook you and fled.
    Even so your sorrow was not for yourself, the betrayed,
    but for them – for us – who betrayed you.
Saviour, we remember your grief
    and we also grieve.

Lord Jesus: You looked upon power
    in the High Priest's house,
    the court of the Procurator.
    And you were silent in dignity, and in grief,
    to see what we men make
    of the power your Father lends us:
    we use it to cheat, lie, work injustice,
    kill the good.

Saviour, we remember your grief
and we also grieve.

Lord Jesus: You looked down from the cross of pain
and grieved
not for yourself
but for those who did wrong
and for the Mother bereaved, and the sorrowing friend.
What others bore
moved your heart to pity,
even while you were bearing the sin of the world.
Saviour, we remember your grief
and we also grieve.

Lord Jesus: we look at your cross.
It accuses us of sin.
It assures us of pardon.
Keep us, Saviour, day by day
in the joy of your salvation;
and, day by day, keep us penitent
as those for whom your heart has bled,
your tears have fallen.
Saviour, we remember your grief
and we also grieve.

11

A Responsive Prayer for Good Friday
– 'His Cross and his Crown'

'. . . The Lamb who was killed is worthy to receive power . . .'
Rev 5:6–14

'As by Thy cross Thou dost restore, So rule. . . .'

Jesus of Nazareth,
King of the Jews:
this day on your cross you won a great victory
over the powers of darkness and death.
You, the Crucified, made of your crucifixion a coronation –
'Did e'er . . . thorns compose so rich a crown?'

Lamb who died, Christ our King,
   we praise you on your royal throne.

We give you glory
for all the multitudes of folk
who have come to the foot of your cross, repented of their
      sin,
believed in you for pardon and new life,
and have become by grace, through faith,
citizens of your kingdom.
Lamb who died, Christ our King,
   we praise you on your royal throne.

We thank you
for your transforming grace at work in the world.
Even in the darkness of what remains to be done,
your reign already brings truth, kindness and healing.
We thank you for martyrs, missionaries, pastors and
      teachers,
saints of prayer and action,
good Christian men and women in high places and
      ordinary jobs
who fly heaven's flag on earth.
Lamb who died, Christ our King,
   we praise you on your royal throne.

We claim your help
for those who stand on your kingdom's frontier,
facing in your strength peril for the body and darkness for
      the soul.
Sustain your Church under persecution;
give wisdom and patience to Christians pursuing justice
      and peace.
Penetrate with your strong grace where we cannot
to tame human violence and check human wickedness.
We pray with confidence that you can conquer all things.
Lamb who died, Christ our King,
we praise you on your royal throne.

Exert your kingly rule
over the illness of our friends,

and the troubles of our neighbours;
with your sceptre break the hardness of our own hearts;
so that all your people
in Spirit and in truth may say,
Lamb who died, Christ our King,
we praise you on your royal throne.

Easter

1

'. . . He is not here – he has been raised! . . .' Mk 15:42 – 16:8

Hallelujah!
Christ is risen – the empty cross no longer bears a dying
      Saviour,
   no longer a dead Master lies in the empty tomb.
   He is not there, he is risen;
     Jesus stands in the garden,
     walks on the road,
     enters the fear-locked room.

Hallelujah!
Christ is risen – people in their Sunday best amid daffodils
   sing hymns higher and louder
   than the Good Friday ones.
     Jesus is risen and we shall rise with him;
     lo, he is with us always,
     even to the end of the age.

But we remember
that the Resurrection
   was at first much more alarming:

women ran frightened from a grave gone wrong
  – though one stayed
    to see Christ
    through her tears;
men were scornful, sunk in remorse and doubt
  – though for two who ran to see
    seeing was believing.
And in the evening when the Master came
his disciples were scared.

And we remember
that the Resurrection
    was accomplished with remarkably little fuss,
    though later there was talk of thunder, earthquake
    – the sort of thing one feels *ought* to have happened.
    In fact
    Christ passed from death to life so quietly
    that he left the grave-clothes undisturbed:
    they lay where he had lain in them.
    Death had no hold upon the Sinless One
    and, his task of dying done,
    he rose *of course*.

Risen Lord, we adore you.
Hallelujah for your rising!

Fill us with the *joy* of the Resurrection:
    make us strong in the certainty of faith,
    and bold to witness.

Fill us with the *terror* of the Resurrection:
    your Father and our Father,
    your life and our life,
    must be taken even more seriously now
    in resurrection light.

Fill us with the *peace* of the Resurrection:
    by your death the love of God went all the way,
    but for your raising
    the power of God
    was not pushed to the limit.
    To save us, your God and our God knew pain

but not strain, not testing
(for that you needed a mortal body
and for that you became flesh).

★

The power which raised you
and holds us
is limitless
and wins of course.

Hallelujah!

2

Greeting at Early Communion

'. . . Good News . . . of the greatest importance . . . that
Christ died for our sins . . . that he was raised to life. . . .'
1 Cor 15:1–1

This is the solemn memorial of Christ's death.
It is also the celebration of his life.

★

Jesus Christ the Crucified is risen. He lives to die no more.
He lives to intercede for us.

★

You ask me how I know he lives?
He lives within my heart.

'Jesus Christ is risen today. Hallelujah'

(This hymn is sung)

So many things happened that day.
It was hard afterwards to be sure of all the details:
some remembered one thing, some another.
But one thing became quite clear – or rather two things:
    yesterday there had been no doubt that he was dead;
    by the end of today, one group of people

was absolutely certain
that he is alive.

3

Call to Worship on Easter Morning

'. . . victory through our Lord Jesus Christ! . . .'
1 Cor 15:54–58

It is Easter and we celebrate life
— the trumpets of the angels,
  the singing of springtime birds,
  and the hallelujahs of the Church
  say *Christ is risen,*
  Jesus lives!

It is Easter and we celebrate victory
— the Christ who died for sin
  is risen in glory,
  the devil is done for
  and the cross rises over the field of battle
  as empty as the tomb,
  and stands for ever as the flag
  of our conquering Lord.

It is Easter and we celebrate hope
— if Christ has been raised
  anything can happen,
  and no good thing is impossible.

Hallelujah!

4

Offertory Prayer

'. . . God loves . . . one who gives gladly.'   2 Cor 9:7

In the joy of the springtime sunshine,
we come to you with gladness.

In the joy of knowing Christ alive,
we come to you with thanksgiving.
In the wonder of knowing
that you can use what we give and what we are,
we bring you these gifts.
Bless them, use them;
bless us; use us
for Jesus Christ's sake.

5

Credal Prayer

'. . . the one whom Moses wrote about in the book of the Law
and whom the prophets also wrote about. He is Jesus . . .'

John 1:45

We remember, heavenly Father, that on the first day of the
week
you raised from death your Son our Saviour Jesus.

We celebrate
your creation of the universe and of the world within it;
your patient teaching and leading of mankind before
history and during history;
your calling of Israel to be your own people, and to be
first among the nations in your friendship;
your intention that through Israel all nations should be
blessed;
your sending of Jesus Christ to proclaim and embody
the good news of your love;
your glory, truth and grace in him made visible and
available;
his going all the way to death in love for us;
your pardon for mankind, which he expressed and sealed
upon the cross of obedience and of pain;
your power in raising him from the dead, never more to
die.

He lives, Hallelujah! He lives
    in the freedom of the resurrection body;
    to intercede always for us as his human brothers and
        sisters;
    to pour the Holy Spirit into all who are his by grace
        through faith;
    to rule over all things from his throne at your right hand,
        till he comes again in glory at the time known only to
        you.

We glory in the greatest thing that has ever happened
    your redemption of the world by the death and rising
        again of the Lord Jesus Christ.

We pray that you may accept our worship and us
    for his dear sake.

6

The Jews

'. . . Jesus Christ . . . was a descendant of Abraham . . .' Mt 1:1–17

God of Abraham and Father of Jesus:
we pray for your people Israel
who, as we see it,
looked for Christ but could not, would not, take
Christ crucified,
and therefore missed the joy
of a risen Lord.

We give thanks for the Jews who did believe:
for Peter, James and John, Mary Mother and Mary
        Magdalene
and all who were with them when Jesus rose
– and for Paul who was not yet with them then.

With Paul we yearn for the conversion of the Jews
and pray for them
    in their sufferings,
    in their genius,
    in their wealth,

in their generosity,
and in their obedience to your word
in the scriptures of law and promise.

Forgive our long lack of love for them;
forgive our easy forgetfulness of what we owe to them;
in your way and your time unite us to them
in the grace and power
of him who came to us in Jewish flesh,
Jesus of Nazareth, Christ our Lord.

7

Light in Darkness

'. . . even darkness is not dark for you . . .' Ps 139:7–12

In resurrection light we pray to you
for all who know deep darkness:
> those who mourn the passing of people they loved,
> or times when they were happy;
> those who are disappointed with life, or with
> themselves;
> those who have given up hope.

Let there be light for them:
not flickering at the end of the tunnel
but now, present and preposterous – the light of life.

Grant them the faith that though death claims all things
and all people,
yet the claim of death shall not be eternally upheld
on anyone redeemed or anything good.
Grant them the faith that can say, smiling,
'I die, but my Redeemer lives, and I shall live with him'.

And,
gracious God,
may our lives help to make that faith
believable;
for Jesus' sake.

8

Responsive Prayers at Easter

'When you pray . . . for something, believe that you have received it . . .'
Mk 11:24

Risen Lord: we thank and praise you
for coming, and living, and dying,
to show what human life was always meant to be.
We adore you for that great love
which brought you to earth
and sent you to the cross
– all the way, for us.
Christ who died, Christ our living Lord
   we praise you in your love and power.

Risen Lord: we bring to you
the world you love and came to save.
Still there are places
where the good news of pardon, peace and new life
has not been heard;
and there are places where it has been heard
often enough,
but never heeded.
We ask you to hurry on the day
when all the world shall become your kingdom
and all people live as your subjects.
Christ who died, Christ our living Lord
   we praise you in your love and power.

Risen Lord: we claim the saving health of your touch
for everyone who is ill or handicapped
in body or mind,
and everyone who is in pain or distress today.
Strengthen with your blessing
all who heal the sick and comfort the dying,
and all who, in palace, house or hut,
contrive to live at peace with their neighbours.
We know you hear our prayer, for you taught us
to pray in that certainty.
Christ who died, Christ our living Lord
   we praise you in your love and power.

Risen Lord: we ask your help
for all who teach and lead the young,
so that, by the rule of your kingdom,
youth may have visions of goodness
and noble unselfish ambition.
We ask your help
for all who still hold fast
in the turmoil of daily business
to the Christian ideals with which they began,
and seek in mature life to keep the childlike heart.
We know you hear our prayer, for you taught us
to pray in that certainty.
Christ who died, Christ our living Lord
we praise you in your love and power.

Risen Lord: be very close today
to the people old and young
who will profess their faith
and put on Christ in baptism.
Give them an unforgettable awareness of your presence,
and grant them grace to rise from the water
as you yourself were raised from death
into newness of life.
We know you hear our prayer, for you taught us
to pray in that certainty.
Christ who died, Christ our living Lord
we praise you in your love and power.

Risen Lord: give the certainty of resurrection faith
to everyone who today is near to death,
to all who nurse the dying,
and to all who mourn.
As Mary wept in the garden
but through her tears saw you,
may they discover that through your victory
in the midst of death they are in life.
We know you hear our prayer, for you taught us
to pray in that certainty.
Christ who died, Christ our living Lord
we praise you in your love and power.

Risen Lord: on Resurrection Day we ask you
to fill again with hope
the minds of all those who are discouraged
or weary in welldoing.
Renew the patience of those
who think and argue, strive and wait
for justice and peace
in Africa and Asia, Europe and America,
India, Sri Lanka and Ireland.
Raise the spirits of our fellow citizens,
and of those who lead us.
Give courage and hope
to attempt great things for you
and expect great things from you.
We know you hear our prayer, for you taught us
to pray in that certainty.
Christ who died, Christ our living Lord
we praise you in your love and power.

9

At the Beginning of Evening Worship

'. . . raised to life three days later . . . he appeared . . .'
1 Cor 15:3–5

Heavenly Father: we are trying to imagine what it was like
that first Easter evening.

They knew that Jesus was alive; at least, many did.
Thomas still held out, refusing to trust the word of others,
refusing to believe what he wanted to believe,
not daring to believe what he wanted to believe.
He so loved the Master, he so dreaded disappointment.
Better to remain in mourning, hugging his memories
for such consolation as they were worth.

There had been other doubters for an hour or two.
Women had rushed back from the early morning vision in
the garden:
some frightened, some tearful, all hysterical,

or so it had seemed to the men.
Who could believe the tale of an empty tomb,
a moved stone, an angel – or was it two angels?
So Peter and John had hurried off to see for themselves;
and they had seen
and believed.

Peter knew he was forgiven: there was peace in that.
John knew his Friend was alive: that was enough for him,
   for now.
The Marys had spent their tears
and sat in passionless, exhausted wonder.

Then came the couple from Emmaus
with a story of conversation
on the road with a stranger who at the tea table
turned out to be Jesus.
Back at once to town in haste
not knowing that the Jerusalem disciples had the news
   already
– a hushed hilarious rivalry of did you know and yes we
   did
and isn't it marvellous?

Now, to complete the luminous and terrible day
which had seen the creation of life the second time round,
Jesus was suddenly there.
No door could keep him out.

He didn't excite them.
He knew they were all tired out with sorrow and joy,
shame and reconciliation.
No more excitement; sufficient unto the day
is the hallelujah thereof.
Just simply 'Peace be with you'
his peace, past understanding.

Lord God, we also have rejoiced in the resurrection.
Now we also wait for the fuller giving of the Holy Spirit
to deepen, widen the river of resurrection life
flowing through the world.
But most of all, now, we need to know

here in the quietness between holy day and holiday
– we need to know that the Lord who was raised from
   death
is with us in newness of life
breathing his peace.

Abide with us,
Lord Jesus.

10

*Opening Prayer
on the Evening of a Spring-like Easter Day*

'It was late that Sunday evening, and the disciples were
gathered together . . .' Jn 20:19–21

Father:
we praise and thank you for today
   its long-awaited warmth and sunshine,
   the people strolling in holiday clothes
   and the happy children.
Even more we thank you
for what the day has meant
to us who believe in the Resurrection of Christ your Son.

★

Lord Jesus:
we have tried to imagine your first friends
in their bewildered desolation
at the fact of your death,
and in the scarcely supportable joy
which began with the sight of an empty tomb
and messages from angels and frightened women.
By evening the truth was starting to penetrate:
you were not there in the tomb
because you had been raised from the dead.

★

Then, only then. . . .
when they had gathered, still nervous

about the Jewish authorities
and the temple police,
and had shut and barred the door. . . .
Then, only then. . . .
as they gathered
and in whispers shared the news,
and their lingering doubts,
and their growing conviction. . . .
Then, only then did you appear to them;
features which they recognised with love,
scars which told them what you had suffered. . . .
Then you came to them
with words of cheer.
Then they were sure.
Then they were glad.

★

Draw near to us as we worship, Lord Jesus,
so that we also may recognise the One slain for us
and risen.
Come to us with words of cheer,
so that we also may be sure
and we also may be glad
in your living presence.
We ask it in your name,
even as we pray in your words:
        Our Father. . . .

11

Petition on Easter Evening
after reading the Emmaus story in Luke 24

'. . . Jesus . . . walked along with them . . .' Lk 24:13–55

Risen Lord and Master:
we ask you to meet us on the road.
Meet us in conversation that opens up the Scriptures.
Meet us in the supplying of our needs.

Meet us in those people whose needs we can supply.
Be made known to us in the breaking of bread.

★

And when days or moods are dark
and the one in whom we had hoped seems far away,
meet and walk with us
for your name's sake.

12

'His Joy and Ours'
A Prayer of Commitment

'. . . because of the joy that was waiting for him . . .'

Heb 12:12

Lord Christ, our Saviour and King:
we glimpse with amazement a love so deep – all
     undeserved –
so deep that it could see in us men and our salvation
something to take *joy* in.
That saving us could be for you
a *joy* worth crucifixion
leaves us silent and adoring at your feet.

★

Lord Jesus, forgive us, restore us and renew us;
transform us into something fit to be called your *joy*!

★

Crucified and risen Lord, you prayed and you promised
that your joy, like your peace, should be fulfilled in us,
in our life, in our experience.
This Easter time waken in us once more
the radiant joy that you alone could win
and you alone can give.
Take and shake your church here in . . .,
and make us a Community of your Resurrection,

a colony of your Kingdom
of love and peace and *joy*!

★

Hear and empower our prayer
for your glory's sake.

LOW SUNDAY

13

The Sunday after Easter: Looking In

'. . . When the festival was over, they started back home . . .'
Lk 2:41, 43, 51–52

Father
we thank you that our life is varied and enriched
by the seasons of the year and the festivals of your Church.
Especially we thank you for those times
when we are cheered and rested by holidays.
We pray for ourselves and for one another
as the busy round of ordinary days begins again
after Easter.

★

Keep us convinced
of the victory of Christ your Son,
which became so vivid for us in the Easter hallelujahs.
Sustain in our minds
the peace renewed in garden or countryside,
as we return to the world of typewriters and telephones.
And in your Church
may the joy of high festival still echo
in the habitual services, meetings and appointments.
May your Holy Spirit turn each week into a holy week,
each Sunday into the Lord's Day of resurrection and new
    life.

14

The Sunday after Easter: Looking Out

'As he saw the crowds, his heart was filled with pity . . .'
Mt 9:36–38

Lord God
in the lingering joy
of resurrection festival
we pray
for everyone who enjoyed Easter
as a Bank Holiday week-end
and seemingly nothing more.
May your mysterious grace work upon all their haphazard
contacts
with your Church that week-end. . . .
the hearing of a remembered hymn,
something on a church notice board,
a newspaper article,
or a programme half watched on television.
May our prayer make some difference to them.

★

Forgive us
if their failure to see the Easter faith
comes from our failure
to show it.

*. . . He ascended into heaven, and sitteth on the right
hand of God the Father Almighty; from thence he
shall come to judge the quick and the dead . . .*

Ascension

1

'. . . he was taken up to heaven as they watched . . .'

Acts 1:9

Great God, there is no end to your power,
nor to the gifts of your grace.
You give life, and then life more abundant;
the table you spread before us is not mere subsistence
but a banquet.

Flowers have to attract insects,
but that they also look lovely to us
is something extra, inessential,
which you have added
making it that much easier
for us to believe.

As you give to living things not merely life
but also beauty,
so to the essentials of faith you add a glory
which makes your invitation to faith
the more persuasive,
like a snare set not to entrap

but to set free our spirit
into belief.

So in the manner of Christ's passing
from human sight,
you give beyond necessity.

Enough surely, that he came in your love,
lived, served, befriended, died, was raised
to set the seal of victory upon it all
– enough in that to save us,
   enough to open heaven to believers.
Yet you add the cloud of glory.

Transfiguration mountain was pure gift,
added *after* Peter had recognised your Son
for what he is.
The day of palms was pure gift,
added *after* the crowd had tried to make him king
as they understood it.

Pure gift also is Christ's Ascension.

You call us to walk by faith, in hope,
but – such is your grace –
not without vision.

We believe
that Jesus Christ, your Son, our Saviour King,
till he return,
has gone to be with you, ruling and interceding;
and to all the reasons for believing
which you have already given
you add this:
that some men saw him go.

2

The King is Back in Power

'. . . I have been given all authority in heaven and on earth . . .'
Mt 28:18

Lord Christ, what do they mean
when they teach us that you ascended into heaven?
Was it not enough that you came down to earth?
showing the Father's glory,
telling the Father's truth;
demonstrating that God in his strength does not bully
and God in his holiness does not humiliate sinners,
but welcomes faith,
    honours repentance,
    renews life.

All your way with us had been humility and gentleness,
majesty set aside – obedience to death
    after submission to man's false justice,
    pardon for your murderers
    even from the cross.

Risen from death, transfigured into freedom –
no door could shut you in or keep you out
– yet you were not robed in frightening splendour;
    friends recognised you
    and there was provision for them
    to go on doing so
    in bread and wine and the empowering Spirit.

After such sufficiency, why do they go on
to tell us you ascended, hands raised in blessing,
through clouds to heaven?
What does it mean?

Perhaps it means you know our weakness, Lord,
you know our need of this last sign
to reassure us
that the majesty you set aside to save
you have taken again to protect the saved.

★

We worship and adore you,
risen, reigning King.
We look for your coming again,
in like manner as they saw you go.
In this royal confidence help us to live, and serve you day
       by day
till faith be sight, and all waiting turn to joy
in the place you have gone to prepare.

3

The Transfiguration of Man

'. . . When anyone is joined to Christ, he is a new being . . .'
2 Cor 5:16–17

Father God, we thank you
for glorifying this temporary world
and this transient life of man,
by sending your Son to live a human life and die a human
   death.

Upon him
rests our deepest certainty and our highest hope;
for having conquered death he rose and ascended,
returning to the majesty he had set aside
for our sake.

Now he reigns
with you and the Holy Spirit
on the throne of the universe;
our Advocate in heaven
just as the Holy Spirit is his representative with us on
   earth.

We thank you for the peace
of knowing that our Saviour
is Lord of all.

We adore him
who once was subject

to human limitations of time
but now is the same yesterday, today and for ever.

We adore him
who was once confined
to a particular place
but now is present
wherever men and women turn to him.

Father,
we ask you in his name
to light up our little lives with your great glory;
raise our thought, imaginations and desires
to the level at which Christ lives.

So may we who believe
live, as he promised we should,
the life of eternity in the here and now.

Forgive our sins
and make us able
to love you with heart and mind and soul and strength,
and to love our neighbours as ourselves;
make us capable of doing good.

Grant us the Spirit of Christ to live by,
as you have given us
the words of Christ to pray with,
saying:
    Our Father. . . .

4

Royal Salute

'. . . We see him now crowned . . .'   Heb 2:9

Lord Jesus Christ:
we praise you in your heavenly glory
– your unimaginable majesty
   which you set aside to come to earth
   and took again when all was accomplished.

You who love and understand us so completely,
and took to heaven a human brow,
reign there
and intercede
and shall return
for us.
Even so come, Lord Jesus.

5

With the children

'. . . continue in the truths that you were taught . . .'
2 Tim 3:14

Thank you, heavenly Father,
for the Christmas story
    of Jesus coming down to earth
    and being born a baby just like us.
Thank you for the gospel stories
    of Jesus making friends,
    teaching people, healing people,
    and putting lost people back
    on a path through life that makes sense.
Thank you for the Easter story
    of Jesus going on obeying you
    and going on loving us,
    even when it meant getting killed;
    and of Jesus coming back to life
    and promising to live with us for ever.
Thank you for the Ascension story
    of Jesus going back to heaven
    to get it ready for us;
    and promising the Holy Spirit
    to keep us in touch with him.
What wonderful things you do!

★

Please forgive us

for taking so little notice of you.
Help us to honour you;
help us to love you and one another the way you want us
        to,
for Jesus' sake.

6

Out of Sight

'. . . and a cloud hid him from their sight . . . They went
    back to Jerusalem, filled with great joy . . .'
Acts 1:9–10, Lk 24:52

It should have had the bleakness of farewell
almost for ever –
heard voice, seen face, grasped hands:
the cloud had taken you.

But, after a moment's delay gazing where you weren't,
snapped out of it by the angels,
they returned to the city
rejoicing!

Somehow those forty days of your unpredictable presence –
seen here, seen there, not seen, seen again
– had acclimatised them
to your absence.

They who had seen you were ready to enter
the blessedness of those who do not see
yet believe, serve, hope, and are prepared
for the Spirit to come when he will.

That day they joined *us*, found the joining joyful,
and invited us to share their expectation of your return
and their certainty meanwhile
of promised Pentecost.

Lord, illuminate by this all our goodbyes
when death or life obliges us
to trust each other
out of sight.

Apply your grace and the mystery of unseen nearness
to mothers of missionaries,
fathers of men of affairs,
and very busy couples.

That you are gone, yet here;
mysteriously present in the Spirit, yet coming again and
   needing to;
pitches a tent of paradox in which, till Paradise,
living is possible.

Thank you, Lord.

7

The Absentee

'. . . it is better for you that I go away' . . . 'Do not hold on to me . . .'
Jn 16:7; 20:17

Lord Jesus:
among all the scenes of your life
this one is different.
Into the other pictures we can walk
by faith and imagination
to find you there.
Scenes by the wayside, tales of the sea. . . .
Even when our pictured Jesus
is disconcerting, or dead,
he seems *there*.
Yes, Lord, even when the Person we see
curses a fig tree or scourges money-changers
or is only a criminal corpse begged by Joseph and
        Nicodemus,
still 'you' are 'there'.

But the point of this Ascension scene
is that you *leave* it
and go away
into the cloud and heaven.

Lord, are you telling us by this

that you are after all in none of them,
our Sunday School wall posters of the mind –
Palestine then and you there, in some imaginary midst?

At Ascension did you go from all the pictures,
from earth as finally as from the tomb?
'He is *not here*; He is . . . *ascended*'?

You are on high
and, to our seeking senses, nowhere else.
You are on high
– Hallelujah!
You are on high
– *Marana tha*, even so, come!

Meanwhile now
our seeking you
must be in neighbour,
    in truth,
    in opportunity and in the Spirit.

And our finding you
must be in the heart.

8

To the uplifted Christ

'. . . To him who sits on the throne and to the Lamb,
be praise and honour . . .'   Rev 5:6–14

Risen and glorious Saviour,
enthroned at the right hand of the Majesty on high:
we join the host of angels
and the multitude which no man can number
of your ransomed saints,
to lift up hearts and voices
in reverent salute.

Lamb slain for us, lifted up to die a shameful death:
we celebrate the love you showed and the victory you won
on that stark cross.
There you kept your promise

to be lifted up as Moses lifted up the serpent in the
   wilderness
 to draw all eyes,
 to draw all men unto you,
 to be the soul-healing and heart-healing
 of all who look up and see you there.

We praise you
uplifted on the cross
to die in duty, mercy, perfect holiness.

We praise you
uplifted now in glory
whence you shall come
to judge the living and the dead;
whence you shall come and call to yourself
those who belong to you in their faith, by your grace.

Be
uplifted day by day in the Church.
We offer ourselves to you
  that our iniquity may be forgiven and our sin purged;
  that soul and body may become a living sacrifice,
  as we offer to God and man
  service which is our reasonable response
  to the love you show
  and the power you promise.

O Christ forgive your Church for her failure to lift you up
in testimony to the world;
for her comfortable parade
of what is not faith,
  nor hope,
  nor love.

O Christ accept in your Church all the simple trust
  and simple goodness
  which is there by your grace.
  Make your Church strong,
  impressive and winsome,
  not for the sake of our good name
  but yours.

*. . . I believe in the Holy Ghost,
the holy catholic Church . . .*

Pentecost

1

'. . . in a few days you will be baptised with the Holy Spirit.'

Acts 1:5

Spirit of God,
moving upon the waters of chaos
to bring order –

Promise of Christ,
making it possible to repent, to believe,
and to know Christ in the heart –

Wind of power and flame of light,
turning cowards into martyrs, the tongue-tied into
    preachers,
making disciples into the Church –

We bless you for your gift of order:
you help us to think,
you help us to pray,
you convince us that history is in God's hands.

We thank you for every time we have found ourselves
    wiser,

or braver, or kinder than we could have been without you;
and for each moment when Jesus our Lord came close to
   us.

We ask you to work in this church:
make us a community, a household in God's family; teach
   us to love.
Make us able to speak the word of God and do the will of
   God

in Christ's name.

2

Picture Language

'. . . my Spirit on everyone . . .'   Acts 2:1–47

Holy Spirit of the living God, we praise you
on the day appointed in the Church
for the remembrance of your coming at Pentecost.

How shall we, can we, dare we speak of you?

When you came upon the Lord Jesus at his baptism
men said you were like
a dove descending:
dove, the gentle bird that is able
to bear messages with sure direction.

When you came at Pentecost men said you were like
a gale of wind, filling the house,
driving the apostles into the street
to speak boldly of new life in Christ:
wind, unseen yet able
to bend tall trees and speed mighty ships.
They said you were like
flames of fire:
flame, insubstantial, not to be grasped or weighed, yet able
to burn, enlighten and empower.

You are he who is most miraculous yet most essential,
most strange yet most ordinary;

it is you who strengthen the martyr and transfigure the
     saint,
yet it is you also who bring the nearness of Christ
to our undramatic awareness
in ordinary and imperfect days.
By you it is
that the Church is brought to shining life
in revival and advance,
and by you it is
that quiet faithfulness survives
in times when great encouragements are denied.
By you it was that the scriptures were given,
and by you that we are enabled to interpret scripture
to each generation.

Soft dove, hot flame, fierce wind
and still, small voice:
you are free and we cannot command you,
but we need you and you are the Father's gift to us.
Come, Holy Spirit, when you will and as you will
     in silent ministry to faith and understanding
     or in the fine rage of revival.
And whenever, however you choose to make yourself felt,
may we be ready to receive you,
and obedient.

We ask it in the name of Jesus,
who gives the words, the Spirit, and the right
to say
     Our Father. . . .

3

Whit Sunday morning

'The Helper will come – the Spirit . . .'   Jn 15:26

Lord God we thank you
that when Jesus was taken from the sight and touch of
  mortal men

those who believed were not left comfortless.
We thank you that they were granted
a continuing awareness of his presence,
and the certainty of your power around them and within.
We thank you for the story of this day:
how the Spirit came
to faithful, prayerful, hopeful disciples.
They said he was like a rushing wind that filled the house;
they said he was like tongues of living flame
    lighting them up one by one;
and people outside were amazed at the difference he made.
When those disciples spoke now about Jesus Christ
their words were bold, forceful, and completely understood
by everyone, even foreigners.
At their first preaching three thousand believed:
the Church grew; persecution and scattering only made it
    grow faster.

★

We thank you
for all that has been transformed,
and all that has been made possible
by your Holy Spirit in the Church.
He has prompted and empowered your people's preaching,
their teaching, their thinking, and their practical kindness.
He has renewed their courage when the way was dangerous
and the going was hard.
Time and again, he has stirred a sleepy Church,
purged a sinful Church,
reinvigorated a tired and timid Church.
We believe he is working in your Church these days,
and we thank you, though with fear.
For it could be
our quiet that he will disturb,
our compromises that he will challenge,
our sins he will judge.
After all,
the day we remember and celebrate was a day of
disturbance.

★

Yet we have no alternative
but to pray the Church's constant prayer
and ask for the Spirit to be poured out.
Give us the courage to bear what it may cost
if your kingdom is to come
and your will be done on earth as it is in heaven.

4

A Family Prayer

'. . . the gift my Father promised . . .'   Acts 1:4–5

Lord Jesus, when Pentecost came
 you kept your Father's promise:
the Holy Spirit arrived.
Your friends who had been frightened
became brave again.
They were in touch with you again,
invisibly but really,
strongly, gladly and for ever.
Give *us* your Holy Spirit, Lord,
to keep us sure of you,
to make us strong and brave
and real friends of yours.
Light up our lives
with your joy, your truth and your kindness,
so that we may shine with your light
for all the world to see.

5

An Offertory Prayer

'Everything . . . in the name of the Lord Jesus . . .' Col 3:17, 23

Almighty God,
Creator of the universe, Saviour of men and Inspirer of the
  Church:

look in mercy, we pray,
upon the Announcements   (Intimations, Notices).
We heard them just now,
and so, unfortunately, did you.
Some of the things we plan
have precious little hope of doing anything
for the spread of your kingdom or the blessing of mankind
– *unless* you come into them and into us.
O God, we need your Holy Spirit
to transfigure the meetings, the clubs and the coffee
   mornings,
the garden parties and the hymn singing.
We need him to transfigure the Offering too.
O God, by your Holy Spirit, come in
and make it all holy;
give us the sense to purge our way of life in the Church
until it *can all* be holy.
We offer now our gifts and ourselves,
for your forgiveness, your transformation, and your use;
in Jesus' name.

6

Petition

'. . . wait for the gift I told you about . . .'   Acts 1:4–5

Give us your Holy Spirit, O God,
as you have promised to all the disciples of Jesus your Son.

★

Dramatically or quietly
give your Spirit of grace so that we may be gracious,
give your Spirit of truth so that we may be truthful,
give your Spirit of might so that we may be strong,
give your Holy Spirit so that we may be holy
in Jesus Christ our Lord.

7

Whit Sunday Evening

'. . . the Holy Spirit came down on them,
        just as on us at the beginning . . .'   Acts 11:15

Lord, what was it like
on the evening of the Day of Pentecost?
Was there a warm glow of achievement?
Of course the apostles gave *you* the credit for the three
            thousand converts:
without your Spirit they'd not have spoken out as they did
– not even Peter;
without your Holy Spirit at work in the listening crowd,
there would not have been the response.
Still, it had been the apostles who witnessed,
Peter's voice that preached the sermon, and,
thanks to you, it had worked.
So was there glory for them that evening
after the last convert had been counselled and gone home
radiant with the joy of sins forgiven?
– a sigh which said, 'The day thou gavest, Lord, is ended',
        'Glory to thee, my God, this night'?

★

Or perhaps it was not like that at all.
Perhaps the apostles were very tired
and, being tired, a little jaded.
Perhaps in the upper room where fire had, so to speak,
            burned
and wind had, so to speak, blown,
there was a feeling of
anticlimax.

Doubt even. Was the morning's enthusiasm too hot to last?
Would it all be a flash in the pan?
True, in their ecstasy they had not been drunk;
but could they, perhaps, have caught the sun?
For it was early summer.

There was sure to be trouble for the new Church.

The authorities could not ignore the disturbance in the
        street:
outdoor orators persuading residents and tourists alike
to believe in a man who – rightly or wrongly –
had been executed as a criminal.

Was there pride, was there doubt, was there fear, Lord?

★

Whichever it was, they needed you
to come in through closed doors as you had before
        Ascension
and say, 'Be of good cheer'.
One thing we know, Lord: you came.
That was the meaning of Pentecost. In your Spirit you had
        come to the believers,
and would never leave them.
However you did it, Lord, you blessed them,
that tired evening of Pentecost.
Before they slept, they knew that you were with them,
giving your grace, your peace, your courage.

★

So come to us, Lord, now.
Meet us in this hour.
Meet us in the words and in the silence,
in declaration and in sacrament;
meet us at the table and be recognised in the breaking of
        bread.
Prompt and answer our prayer,
for we pray in your name.

8

A Whitsun prayer for other times

'. . . some of the spirit I have given you . . .' Num 11:1–30

It was not only to the apostles on the Day of Pentecost
that you came, O Holy Spirit, nor only in Jerusalem;
not there alone, not only then.

★

You had come to men and women before
giving holiness to priests,
vision and voice to prophets,
authority to judges,
courage and charisma to heroes and heroines,
power to kings.
You had been in Abraham and Moses, Gideon, Saul and
          David,
You had spoken through Amos and Isaiah, Ezekiel and
          Malachi.
You had come upon the earth at creation,
and upon Mary when it was time for Messiah to be born.
You had come upon John like fire
and upon Jesus like a dove.

★

And afterwards, and often,
again you came to men and women:
in Samaria they saw you descend on the believers,
at Caesarea, in Antioch and Ephesus.

★

We worship and adore you, Holy Spirit,
promised gift of God, promise so often kept,
even to us;
come, not so much that we may be aware of you,
rather that we may be aware of Christ,
and that we may come to the Father through him.

★

We need you, Holy Spirit
if we are to have
     eyes that see,
     hearts that love,
     minds that understand,
     wills that obey,
     and hands that work
as God ordains.

★

We need you not just at Whitsuntide,
nor just in churches which go in for that kind of thing.
To be the Church at all we need you,
for without you
     we are nothing,
     we know nothing,
     and can do nothing.

★

Come, Holy Spirit,
here and now,
everywhere and for ever;
so that the love of God may work
in the world of men
through Jesus Christ our Lord.

I believe . . . in the communion of saints;
the forgiveness of sins; the resurrection . . .;
and the life everlasting.

Trinity

1

'The grace of the Lord Jesus Christ, the love of God, and
the fellowship of the Holy Spirit . . .'   2 Cor 13:14

Heavenly Father:
we look and worship.
The meadow flower somehow survives and blooms for a
        day,
the unaccounted sparrow flies and falls.
And it is not only man
who recognises beauty, keeps count after all, and mourns.
A child, in search of something, finds a friend,
but even sooner finds a God to hear his prayer.
He who has eyes to see exclaims,
        'The Father loves!'

Holy Spirit:
we think and worship.
Days follow in even pace,
stars circle the pole and planets are predictable;
two squared is almost certain to be four;
iron and feather feel the same pull down to earth;
the human pulse beats to music learnt before birth;

the brain of ant, bee, elephant and man comes ready
        programmed for its life's business;
poet, prophet and child are given words to speak which
        startle and compel.
He who has ears to hear admits,
    'The Spirit moves!'

Christ Jesus:
we love and worship.
There is a Man whose life answered and still answers
mankind's question and quest, our longing and our lack:
the self-despairing begin to hope, and know they are
        forgiven;
the lost find destiny, direction, and a home;
the blind see sense, the deaf hear harmony;
the heart which thought it could not love beats warm again
and sighs, content,
    'My Saviour is God's Son!'

Creation is a fact,
order is recognizable,
and redemption occurs.
In them one God commands, one Spirit breathes, one Love
        reaches out.

When doubt dissolves and faith is given to us,
there is only one thing to be said:
    'My Lord and my God!'

2

From Looking to Meeting

'. . . O Lord, our Lord, your greatness is seen in all the world!'
                                                            Ps 8

O God
we look up and see
your handiwork in the vault of heaven,
the depths of space, the blazing suns and wheeling planets;
in cloud and mountain, snow and scree,

in the spreading trees and the fertile green of meadows,
we see what you have made.
Birds, beasts, insects and fish are your creatures;
we marvel at their form,
and the fitness they have evolved for the life they must
    lead.
It all seems to speak
your love and care for your creation.
For us too you have provided what we need,
for life and also for enjoyment;
we, each in our own life,
have felt your guidance and sometimes glimpsed your
    purpose.
As we think of all this, there can be no other name
for us to call you, in all your might and majesty
and in your meticulous love,
but *Father*.

O God
we realise
that some men and women live nearer to the truth than
    others –
or at least that some seem better than others
at telling us the truth.
In pictures, words and music and all crafts,
there are those whose work speaks to us
with such convincing strength that we say,
'They are inspired'.
Poet and prophet, artist and saint,
speakers of truth and doers of good,
leaders of men and raisers of laughter:
something of you has moved in them
and brought your truth to us.
Even to us have come moments of insight,
wisdom itself sometimes, and then we have felt your touch.
The faith by which we believe,
the grace by which we have occasionally done a little good,
they are not from us, but from you.
That we can speak with you in prayer,
that we can feel sure you are listening,

that we can know the presence of departed Jesus –
what can explain such things but that you come to us
as *Spirit*?

O God
we meet
a man who lives a human life and dies a human death.
His words are without guile,
his thoughts without malice,
and his conduct without sin.
When he speaks, it is truth.
When he acts, it is kindness.
We see him, and know that we have seen you;
in his death we can believe you accept atonement for our
    sin;
in his rising we can believe that you invite mankind into
    eternal life;
he calls you Father and tells us to do the same.
What can it mean but that you have come to us
in the *Son*?

O God
Father, Giver of life,
Spirit, Breath of life,
Christ the Son, Lord of life,
we adore you.

3

The Salute

'. . . the one who sits on the throne . . .'   Rev 21:5–7

Lord God, we salute you as our *Creator*:
    you made the universe and every created thing –
    gases and rocks, microbes and men.
    You have given us life
    and everything that makes us glad to be alive.

Lord God, we salute you as our *Saviour*:
> By ourselves we had lost our way,
> lost our innocence,
> lost our vision,
> lost hope.
> Then you came in Christ.
> In him you show us what you are
> and what you can make us be.
> In him you offer love, forgiveness, and healing.

Lord God, we salute you as our *Renewer*:
> you have poured your Holy Spirit into human hearts.
> He enables us to respond to your love in Christ.
> He enables us to have faith,
> to profess faith,
> and to live the life of faith.

Lord God, we thank you for the Church:
> its fellowship, its teaching and its size –
> the millions on earth and in heaven
> who are our brothers and sisters in Christ.

Lord God, we thank you for calling us together for
> worship,
> these people,
> in this place,
> now.
> Forgive our sins,
> and renew our certainty of being forgiven.
> Accept the offering of our attentive thought.
> Strengthen and bless the people who, in word and
> action,
> will declare your gospel and their faith

> through Jesus Christ our Lord.

4

The Focus

'Israel, remember this! The Lord – and the Lord alone – is our God.'
Deut 6:4

Father, Son and Spirit, your ancient word stands:
you are, and you are One.
Thank you for this blessed and awful simplicity.

★

We make life so complicated, and often complication can't
        be helped
– responsibilities at work conflict with responsibility to
        home, and to church;
– varied interests invite us: world news and local events,
     a good book, a new play,
     such nice neighbours, such a marvellous holiday.
In all these directions our interest goes out,
and our concern: will they like it?
     can we afford it?
     who will win?
So we are pulled all ways at once,
our thoughts and feet dash hither and thither.
And so they should, for you intend us to live thoroughly.

★

Yet with what joy we hear from time to time
your Son's voice: 'You are anxious about many things;
     only one thing is needful –
     choose the better part.'
Help us to choose it, O God, to obey the master-command
so simple, so complete:
     to love you with heart, mind, soul, strength,
     and one's neighbour as oneself;
     to do justly, love mercy, and walk humbly with you.
Incline us to the high and demanding simplicities
which can give meaning and peace
to our fragmented life.
Thank you for them, Lord God.

Grant now the strong blessing of your simple peace.
We do not ask to be rid
of the things and people that matter to us,
the web of linked responsibilities which is our duty.
But take from us
the sense of confusion,
the feeling of unmeetable demands from all sides.
Set us free
from worrying about problems we are not called upon to
        solve,
and outcomes we cannot affect.
Renew our first and highest love for you,
and set all our duties in right order and proportion
around our simple duty to you.
Enable us, constantly loving you and our neighbour,
to go with quiet efficiency to the next task
and then the next,
knowing that you will give the needed strength
for each moment as it comes.
Uphold us in the Spirit of Jesus
who taught us when we pray to say:
        Our Father. . . .

5

A Prayer about Words

'Before the world was created, the Word already existed . . .' Jn 1:1

Thank you, God,
for putting tongues in our heads,
so that we can talk
and tell stories,
say poems
and sing songs.
Thank you for giving us
stories which are full of your truth,
poems which are full of your love
and songs which are full of your glory.

★

Thank you for the good words
which tell us that people care:
'Good morning; how are you?',
'Glad you're better now',
'Come to tea'.
Thank you for the good words
which tell us that *you* care:
'Jesus loves me, this I know',
'God so loved the world
that he gave his Son'.

★

Forgive us, Lord God,
for the unkind words
that we say when we're cross
or talking to people we don't like;
words which hurt
even when we don't really mean them.

★

Help us to use words
as Jesus did:
to bring ourselves and other people
nearer to you.

6

A Prayer about Sunday

'On Sunday . . . we gathered together . . .'   Acts 20:7

It is Sunday,
the first day of the week,
your special day, Lord Jesus,
the day you rose from the dead.

God our Father,
we praise and thank you

for all your good gifts to us:
for life and health,
friends and pleasure,
for work and all interesting things.

Holy Spirit of God,
come into our minds
and help us to understand;
come into our hearts
and help us to love.

O God, Father, Son and Holy Spirit,
inspire and accept our worship,
for it is our highest duty
and our dearest joy,

and we offer it to you
in the name of Jesus.

7

About Sin and Forgiveness

I

'. . . We plead on Christ's behalf: let God change you
from enemies into his friends!'   2 Cor 5:19–21

Thank you, Lord Jesus,
for all the times
when we have made it up after a quarrel.
Thank you for all the times
when we have said 'Sorry'
after being naughty or unkind.
Thank you for the happy feeling
that we are friends again;
thank you for the happy feeling
of being forgiven.

★

Lord Jesus, we believe
that when we make it up again
and forgive one another,
it is because you help us to;
because some of your wonderful love
has come in
to replace the bit of our own love
which we had lost.
Lord Jesus, we depend on you
to make it up for us with God
your heavenly Father,
for all the things we have done wrong.
Help us to trust and love you,
so that we may for ever be friends with God
because of you.

II

'When I was a child . . . ' 1   Cor 13:11

Holy Father, God of all goodness:
forgive our faltering attempts to speak with the children
about deep matters.
We are grown up and we know that sin
is more than being naughty,
that man's rebellion against you
is more than a tantrum,
and that evil has eaten deep
into the fabric of the world
and the quality of our lives.

★

In our hearts' silence we confess
that thought, word and action
have fallen short of the standard
set before us in Jesus Christ.
In our defence we plead nothing
except that Jesus loves us,
that Jesus died for us,

that he is our advocate
at your heavenly throne.

For his sake forgive us,
and by his grace reinforce in us
the will and the ability
to do good;
for the sweetening of the world
and the glory of your name.

9

An Evening Prayer: Thy Kingdom Come

'On the Lord's day the Spirit took control of me . . .'
Rev 1:10

'The day in whose clear-shining light
All wrong shall stand revealed,
When justice shall be throned in might,
And every hurt be healed. . . .'

For *that* day O Lord our God, we yearn
here, as we pray in the evening of a very ordinary day
when the papers have reported the usual mixture
of injustice rampant, war feared and actual,
and many a hurt *un*healed.

Yet, O God, for us who believe, who are in the secret
of your Son's victory and everlasting life,
it has not been an ordinary day;
for it has been the Lord's Day, yours and his,
made for us vibrant with joy and hope
through the presence and power
of your Holy Spirit.

We have been celebrating the message of Christ
in the gladness of Christ;
we have paused in our busy, anxious lives
to remember your love which surrounds us,

your heaven which awaits us,
and the mercies which even now you grant
to the children of men.

Even today, here and there in the world you love,
some wrongs have been righted, some justice done,
some of the hungry have been fed, some of the sorrowful
    cheered,
some fears allayed, some quarrels made up.
And this is only a beginning.

Thank you, God, that your kingdom is beginning to come.
Make *us part* of its coming;
help us to be among those who play fair,
who make peace, who practise charity.
Forgive our sins
and set us free from their power
to beguile us again.

Lord God, our King and Father:
make us more and more your people,
your willing servants and your children
through Jesus Christ our Saviour,
in whose name and words we pray –
    Our Father. . . .

Harvest Festival
Thanks and Offering

1

A Bidding or Call to Worship

'As long as the world exists, there will be a time for
planting and a time for harvest . . .'   Gen 8:22

This is a festival of dependency
–   we depend on God for life and livelihood;
    God depends on us for responsiveness and obedience.

This is a festival of gratitude
–   we thank God for his gifts;
    and we thank one another for helping him to produce
      them.

This is a festival of faithfulness
–   God has kept faith with us,
    fulfilling the ancient promise
    that while the earth remains
    seedtime and harvest shall not cease;
    with our thanks we pledge our faith
    in God's mercy which we receive through Jesus,
    and our faithfulness
    in his service.

This is a festival of sharing
– mankind must share the fruits of the earth,
just as God shares with mankind the task
of making the earth fruitful.

2

A Prayer about Reality in Worship

'. . . They treat your words as simple songs . . .'

Ezek 33:30–32

Forgive us,
loving and merciful Father,
if in our worship we talk nonsense which we feel to be
        appropriate,
saying things to you which we would never dream of
        saying
to one another.

★

Perhaps it does not matter very much
if we sing to you about ploughing fields and scattering seed
when we and you know perfectly well
that none of us, or almost none of us, ever does these
        things.
After all, what we mean is clear,
always supposing we mean it –
that whatever mankind achieves, in agriculture or anything
        else,
it is you who give the increase,
it is you upon whom we still depend
and always shall.

★

But give us your grace
to quicken our wits in worship,
and keep our piety intelligent.

Then we shall not lightly say, 'Forgive us',
for we realise it means we must forgive.
We shall not even say, 'Thank you, Lord' lightly,
for we know it means that we must share your gifts
    and we know it also means
      that things we have worked for and earned are still
        your gifts,
    and we have not deserved them.

★

In this Harvest Festival,
and in all our praise and prayer,
help us by your Holy Spirit
to mean what we say
in Christ's name.

3

Thank You
A Prayer for Leader and Children to say line by line

'. . . What a rich harvest your goodness provides! . . .'
                                 Ps 65:9–13

Thank you, God, for the harvest;
for farmers and gardeners
ploughing and digging,
tending and reaping the crops,
breeding flocks and herds and chickens.
Thank you for fishermen, miners and oilmen
who live dangerously
to feed and warm us.
Thank you for businessmen,
sailors and airmen,
and those who drive lorries and trains
bringing the food to our shops.
Thank you for shopkeepers,
check-out girls and roundsmen;
and for people who cook meals and lay tables
and do the washing up.

★

Forgive us, heavenly Father,
for taking it all so much for granted –
all this work that people do,
and your miraculous gifts
of soil and frost, sunshine and rain,
and the mystery
of growth and ripening.

★

Forgive us also
for the times we have been selfish
with the things that you have given.

★

Help us to see the wonder of it all;
show us how to help hungry people
to have their fair share
for Jesus' sake.

4

A Prayer of Thanks and Offering
A Prayer for Leader and Children to say line by line

'. . . I have given it to the Levites, the foreigners, the
orphans and the widows, as you commanded me to do . . .'
Deut 26:1–15

Heavenly Father, we thank you
for your gift of food:
for what is grown in gardens
and what is grown on farms
– grain and vegetables,
  flowers and fruit
  and root crops;
  beef and bacon,
  pork and lamb,
  rabbit, poulty and game,

  eggs and milk.
We thank you for what we can grow ourselves;
and we thank you for farmers and fishermen,
market gardeners and stockmen,
shepherds and scientists, traders,
and all the people who make sure
that we get what we can't grow.

★

We don't plough the fields and scatter
but *somebody* has to
and they *do*;
so we are not hungry.
Thank you God.

★

Now, O God, we offer
three kinds of gift to you.

Please take our gifts of *food*,
and make them useful;
may they cheer up the people
who receive them tonight
as presents from the church and from you.

Please take our gifts of *money for the church*;
and make the church wise
in using what we give.

Please take our gifts of *money for the missionaries*
and use them – the money and the missionaries
– to help hungry people in places far away
to grow more food.

★

So we say 'Thank You'
and give our gifts.
Bless the gifts
and bless us
for Jesus' sake.

5

A Prayer of Offering: We Give to the Church

'Every Sunday . . . some money, in proportion to what he has earned.'
1 Cor 16:2

To you who are our life
we give back a little of our livelihood.
To you who in Christ have given us all things
we give back this.
Together in church
we share the gladness of giving.
The gifts are much or little
as you have prospered us much or little,
but the joy and the love and the thankfulness
in which we give
are one and the same.

★

Bless gifts and givers
for Jesus' sake.

6

A Prayer of Offering: We Give to Overseas Aid

'Be generous and share your food with the poor . . .'
Prov 22:9

We who are sometimes a little hungry
offer our gift for those who starve.
We who mostly enjoy life
offer our gift for those who go in fear.
O God, stretch our gifts to serve them,
stretch our minds to imagine
and our hearts to love,
through Jesus Christ our Lord.

I believe . . . in the communion of saints;
the forgiveness of sins; the resurrection . . .;
and the life everlasting.

All Saints
and For the Church

1

'If our hope in Christ is good for this life only . . .,
then we deserve . . . pity . . .'   1 Cor 15:12–22

God:
you are not mocked
nor do you mock your creatures
with false hope.

You have set eternity in man's mind;
You will not then shut mankind out of eternity
like children staring through shop windows
at good things they can never have.

We yearn for the full growth
of powers we already partly possess:
we love after a fashion, partially understand, can create
    something.
The plant pressing up through earth to the warmth which
    draws it
shall not be disappointed in the sunshine.

Why else did Jesus your Son comfort us by saying

there are other rooms in your house, prepared for us,
where we may be with him?

Why else are the runners in Christ's race encouraged
with the thought of giving pleasure to an encompassing
    crowd
of heavenly spectators?

And shall we who have been fed and led
by those who wrote scripture and taught the Church
never be able to meet and thank them?

No wishful dream, John's talk of multitudes
innumerably rejoicing
and praising God together.

For all there is to do and can be done
by human spirits in human fellowship,
life is too short.

The body droops and wastes, its time runs out,
but if *our* love and longing obstinately hold on,
what shall be the grasp of the love of *God* who made us?

Without forgiveness we know we sinners cannot have
heaven's glory or love's reunion;
but these things God would not offer to the penitent
with such explicit mercy,
then not give.

What Father would hold out such gifts as these, to snatch
    away again,
what Brother would tease mortals with talk of everlasting
    life,
what truthful Spirit strike a lying seal in human trust?

Glory to you, O Father God, Creator Spirit,
for your promises which are pledged to us who believe
in Jesus Christ.

2

Cloud of Witnesses
After reading from Hebrews 11 and 12

'. . . you were eternally God, and will be God for ever.'

Ps 90:2

Lord God, you are from everlasting to everlasting;
you lay long plans and keep long promises;
the promise you first made to Abraham
you still honour with those who walk like him in faith;
through your servant Moses you were already beginning
the work which your Son Jesus would perfect;
and your mercy is from generation to generation
upon those who love you.

★

We give you honour and thanks
for the faith and faithfulness of your saints
who . . . (years/centuries) ago first brought together
the stones of which this church was built:
not just the material stone, wood, brick and mortar
for a sanctuary and a shrine,
but the love of God and man
and the fellowship in Christ's Spirit,
which alone is the Church,
built upon the coming and living, the dying and rising
of Christ
who is its only true foundation.

★

And for all who have followed where our fathers led,
pastors and people,
those too, who, at your bidding
have in this association   (diocese, district, area etc.)
proved themselves pastors of pastors
under the One Shepherd
        for all these we give thanks
        and accord them pious memory.

★

Glory to you, O God,
for all who in this place and because of this church
have heard the challenge of your judgment
and the comfort of your grace
as the gospel of Christ has been preached;
and for all who have responded
in the commitment of Christian baptism
and the disciplines of Christian living.

★

May your blessing rest
upon pastor and people in these present days.
May the worship of this place bring you honour,
and may the loving service of these folk to their neighbours
do a work of witness and care
that shall extend your kingdom in many hearts.

Hear us as we pray
for our brothers and sisters in Christ
throughout our own land.
May your Church in all its denominations
minister to the nation's life,
and help to thrust the roots of that life
deep into your creative and redeeming love
which is the ground of our being.

★

And look in mercy
on the Christian Church
in all those parts of the world
where it is dangerous to profess the faith.
Make haste to lead your people out of affliction,
but while perils remain
hold your children steadfast in Christian hope
    until the day dawns
    and goes on for ever
    in the heaven which you have prepared
    for those who believe and endure.

All these thanksgivings we offer
and all these prayers we make
in the one worthy and precious name
of Jesus Christ your Son, our Saviour.

3

God's People, God's Purpose

'. . . We must grow up in every way to Christ, who is the head . . .'
Eph 4:11–16

Father of all mercies:
we thank you for the gifts of your grace
throughout the . . . years of this church's life.
We thank you for ministers and deacons,
teachers and helpers,
those talented in the administration of business,
and those skilled in Christian friendship and hospitality.

★

And we thank you for the undramatic faithfulness
of those never called to lead,
but whose quiet witness
    and prayer
    and kindness
have been channels also for your blessing.

★

We thank you for wisdom and patience
given to your people in times of difficulty,
and for energy and initiative
shown in days of opportunity.

★

We give thanks for the growing sense of oneness
among the churches
of this town and district;
and we pray that in years to come
the gospel of reconciliation

may sound with new clarity and power
from a united Christian community,
to the glory of your name
and the blessing of many.
We ask it through Jesus Christ our Lord.

4

Prayer in the Place of Meeting

'. . . not . . . on this mountain or in Jerusalem . . .'

Jn 4:19–24

God and Father of Jesus Christ:
you have taught us by your Son that it is in no temple,
no appointed holy place, that you are to be found
by the seeking heart –
>   not in Jerusalem, not on Mount Gerizim,
>   but in spirit and in truth.

★

Yet in your kindness you allow us to have special places
        and times
at which it seems easier to meet you.
To the children of Israel, travelling the desert
between Egypt and the Promised Land,
you gave a tent.
Whenever their march halted
they pitched the Tent of Meeting, where they could expect
to offer their prayers and receive your blessing.

★

This church is such a tent:
no more holy, scarcely more permanent,
not to be confused with your real dwelling
in eternity and the believer's heart,
but a help,
a place meanwhile to meet one another
and you.

★

We thank you for every church where we have heard you
      speak,
where we have seen your love in the welcome of our
      friends
and gained your peace when we were troubled.

★

We thank you for *this* place of meeting,
for the years   (centuries)
of devotion and Christian effort
centred in this spot,
and for the saints who prayed
where now we pray.

★

The very walls speak their own impermanence, and efface
      themselves:
'*God* is love', 'Sir, we would see *Jesus*',
'*Jesus Christ* the same yesterday, today and for ever'.

★

Save us from idolatry of place;
cast out the evil triviality
which says that *only here* – in this building,
      this pew,
      this way – will I worship.
But still challenge and inspire us, comfort and strengthen
      us
by the memories and loyalties which cluster here.
As Haran was to Abram, as Bethel to Jacob,
so let this building be to us –
a way-station on a longer journey than the road to church.

So we come
as we usually, or always, or sometimes do,
to this place now,
with a remembering awareness of our days:

a week – or longer – of life, work, tension, friendship,
things we are satisfied with
and things we are ashamed of,
cause for thanksgiving,
and reasons for regret and shame and fear.
We come as children to our Father,
counting on your understanding,
begging your pardon,
sure of your love.
We come seeking courage and seeking truth,
seeking grace,
not for ourselves only; we come representing
those who cannot, those who will not, come,
our rulers, servants, comrades,
the children, the elders and the ill.
For us and them
we seek the blessing not of the shrine
but of its God.

5

The Imperfect Church

'. . . I saw the Holy City, the new Jerusalem . . .' Rev 21:2

O God:
your long and forgiving faithfulness to Christ's Church
is one of the marvels of history.

★

We have preached your Gospel, and perverted it;
we have evangelised the four corners of the world,
    and mumbled prayers over men who exported liquor,
      traded opium,
        and imported slaves.
We have tried to do good
and succeeded in doing a fair amount of evil as well.
We have fed the hungry and burned the heretic;
we have practised Christian love and nourished petty
        resentment.

We are full of faith and fickleness,
    hope and hypocrisy,
    love and lies.

★

Yet – such is your grace
– you have pardoned the Church and renewed her power,
you have blessed her witness and authenticated her
        ministry.
You have honoured the people
    who have too often dishonoured you.
Your way is wonderful, heavenly Father,
so to forgive and use
such an imperfect instrument.

★

Let your mercy chasten us, O God,
not make us complacent;
let us not sin that grace may abound.
The world needs the holiness you give
to those who will let themselves be made holy.
Purge and cleanse the Church.
Make us to be what you have called us to be:
the recognisable and active Body of Christ.

★

Get yourself glory now and always in the Church
through Jesus Christ
the Lord of the Church.

6

The Changing Church

'To him who by . . . his power working in us is able to do so much
more than we can ever ask . . .: to God be glory in the chuch . . .'
Eph 3:20–21

Thank you, Lord Jesus,
for calling us to be your Body the Church.
Thank you for healing us and making us more ourselves
    through the give and take of Christian fellowship.
Thank you for the way in which what we have learnt
    and thought about in church
    has enabled us to realise
    our vocation to your service in everyday life.
Thank you for every occasion
    when we have spoken and acted together
    as a Christian community.

Forgive us for all our failures
to be the church we ought to be:
    our failure to be loving
    and open with one another;
    our failure to relate what we do on Sunday
    to what we do with the rest of the week;
    our failure to project,
    in neighbourliness towards the world around us,
    the faith which we share here.

Help us to see how we ought to change;
keep us patient with one another.
Help us to see the church without illusions, admitting its
        faults,
but help us also to recognise the hopeful signs
which already point in the direction
of what the church ought to become.

Help us to become what we profess to be, and want to be;
but also accept our thanks for all your grace
in making us what we are already.

Give us courage, vision and love;

give us your Holy Spirit to guide us into all truth,
for your name and glory's sake.

7

The Witnessing Church: Responsive Prayer

'. . . you are . . . chosen to proclaim the wonderful acts of God,
who called you out of darkness into his own marvellous light . . .'
1 Peter 2:4–10

God and Father: we thank you for the grace given to this
church during . . . years; for those who by your grace have
proclaimed the Gospel here, and those who by your grace
have believed and entered into eternal life. We ask you to give
us who follow them the same faith and the same faithfulness.
O Lord our God
    accept our thanks and hear our prayer.

We praise you for the courage and hope in which the men
and women of . . . (year) came together to establish this
church. We thank you for the generations which have continued what they began – praying, working and sacrificing,
so that the church and its message might be ours also. Keep us
faithful like them in praying and in doing and in giving.
O Lord our God
    accept our thanks and hear our prayer.

Father, we thank you for great goodness in ordinary people,
the people whose presence has made a congregation, whose
voices have swelled the singing, whose 'Amen' has resounded
to the prayers, and whose love has created a fellowship. May
your Holy Spirit flow richly into us as a people now, so that
we may continue in a devotion and a friendship from which
none may feel excluded or exclude themselves – all one in
Christ Jesus.
O Lord our God
    accept our thanks and hear our prayer.

God and Father of us all: we thank you for the increasing
unity of your Church in this town (city, village), and for

the part we have been able to play in the life of the whole people of God here, through the Council of Churches. We bless you for every Christian thing we have been able to do together; grant that we may go on to live more and more as part of the one Christian Church in . . . (place). We ask this so that we may be encouraged and so that Christian witness may be strengthened.

O Lord our God
accept our thanks and hear our prayer.

Spirit of light and truth: we thank you for all those who down the years have led and taught the young in this church, and have served you in the joyful ministries of music, dance, drama and entertainment. In all our practice of all the arts, help us to remember and demonstrate the presence of our Saviour, so that all we do and attempt may be to God's glory, in God's Spirit, through God's Son.

O Lord our God
accept our thanks and hear our prayer.

REMEMBRANCE SUNDAY

1

A Bidding: Reasons for Silence

'Be silent, everyone . . .'   Zech 2:13

Let us keep silence because God is our Judge.
The prophet Zechariah says:
'Be silent, everyone, in the presence of the Lord'.

Let us keep silence, as people are silent
when they have been stunned by some great shock
    as the world is stunned by the constant eruptions
    of violence and war;
    as the survivors are stunned after battle
    or a terrorist attack.

Let us keep silence because we need a respite
from the clamour
of opinion, desire and persuasion.

Let us keep silence out of respect for the dead.
Millions have died, in two great wars and many lesser ones;
we are alive in the world they have left us,
in nations they thought they were defending for us.

Remembering the dead of two world wars,
remembering the continued daily toll of human life,
seeking the mercy of God for those who mourn,
and praying for peace in our time,
let us keep silence. . . .

2

After the Silence: I

'The world and all that is in it belong to the Lord;
the earth and all who live on it are his.'   Ps 24:1

O Lord our God:
the earth is your creation and we are your children.
Forgive us for the history of wrong
in which your children have killed one another
and spoiled your world.

Hear our prayer
for the people who still mourn loved ones killed in war,
and for those who still suffer from wounds received in war.
Hear our prayer for nations in which there is no peace
    today,
and for nations which are at odds with themselves
through internal tensions.

Teach us the ways of peace: cure the rich nations
of the folly of the arms race.

Teach us the ways of justice: lest the tension between rich
    nations
and poor ones break out in our worst wars yet.

★

Draw us all in heart and mind
nearer to him who came as Prince of Peace,
Jesus Christ your Son our Saviour.

3

Bidding before the Silence

'. . . The brave soldiers have fallen . . .' 2 Sam 1:19, 25, 27

In the peace of this place and this day,
let us quietly remember those who since 1914 have gone
        forth to war
as our fellow citizens, and in our name, and did not return.

Let us remember also those who came back with their lives,
but had their bodies maimed or their minds damaged;
and the men and women who sustained no measurable
        injury
but can never forget the pain, the shock and loss
of battle.

Let us remember the bereaved,
not forgetting that in modern warfare we have to mourn
not only men and women who die in uniform,
but civilians dead in bombing and bombardment
and in the starvation and pestilence of devastated lands.

Let us remember the dead
whom war, and their duty as they saw it, made our
        enemies:
our brothers and sisters from Germany, Italy and Japan;
with loving and fearful thought also
for those on both sides who died deep in anger and cruel
        zest.

Let us remember the thousands who this day, throughout
     the world,
will know fear and suffering, and meet death
in the wars which have not ended.

In our hearts let us confess the prejudice and hatred
which still possess us – our share in warmongering,
our continuous contribution to the world's conflicts.

Let us give thanks for sacrifices made for us
though we did not deserve them,
and let us ask forgiveness for our failure
to be children of peace.

Let us give thanks for the measure of peace we now enjoy,
for the survival so far of the nation which means most to us,
and for God's hitherto unending patience and mercy
toward our foolish and sinful race.

Let us keep silence:
     in thankfulness,
     in pity,
     in shame,
     and in the renewed resolve
     to love and be at peace.

4

After the Silence: II

'. . . He will be called . . . "Prince of Peace".'   Is 9:6

O God: we thank you for the humbling memory of all who
     have
suffered turmoil and pain in hope of guarding what we
     treasure,
and in hope of bringing peace.
We pray for those who still bear the sadness of loss, or who
     live
crippled lives, as the price of what we call our victories.
We offer ourselves to be the instruments of your peace,

and the witnesses to your love.
Give peace in our time, O God,
through him who is called the Prince of Peace,
your Son Jesus Christ our Lord.

5

To Say with the Children

'. . . be courageous, all you that hope in the Lord.'

1 Tim 6:12

Thank you God
for brave people:
lifeboat crews
who save people in stormy seas;
firemen
who rescue folk from burning;
miners and fishermen
and all whose daily work is dangerous.

Thank you for another kind of bravery:
the bravery of people ill and handicapped
– blind, deaf, dumb and lame,
– and all who put a brave face
on a difficult life.

Thank you for the people who were brave in war,
especially those who died bravely
defending our country.

★

Heavenly Father,
help us all to be brave
when we need to be;
but please spare us
from having to be brave
in another war.

Teach us to fight bravely

for peace and fairness,
for righteousness and truth;
through Jesus Christ our Lord.

A STATEMENT OF FAITH

'. . . Be ready . . . to answer anyone who asks you to
explain the hope you have . . .'   1 Peter 3:15

We believe in God
who, in his Son Jesus Christ,
has come among us to defeat the power of sin
and the fear of death.

We believe in God the Holy Spirit,
poured out upon the Church
to assure it of the presence and power
of the risen Christ.

We believe
that before time was, God is;
and that when history shall be ended and the universe
    scrapped,
God is,
ever the same loving Father
who has stooped to include us, through Christ,
in his everlasting purpose.

We believe
that God rules the future as well as the past,
and that nothing takes him by surprise.

Changing times
can change the way God's truth has to be told
– and no human words have ever told it right.
But truth is not in human telling.

The truth is Christ
as our life is Christ
and our hope is Christ.

In him we hope,
though all else change,
though all else be taken from us.

We trust him
to guide us and the Church

to what we must become;
and we trust him for strength
to do what we and the Church must do.

Our hope is in God
who raised Jesus Christ from the dead
and calls us to new life in him.

Our hope is in God
who made the universe of space and time
and will replace it with eternity.

Our hope is in God
for today,
for tomorrow,
and for ever.

To him be glory.

AMEN.

INDEX OF PRAYERS

Listed with keynote text, main source reference, and
sequence of secondary references

ADVENT

CHRISTMAS

LENT

Jn 12:21, 20:29/ Mk 9:5–6 cf Lk 9:33, Mt 14:25–33, Lk 22:61/ 1 Cor 15:5–8, 1 Jn 3:2

III '. . . the chosen race, the King's priests, God's own people . . .' 1 Pet 2:9
1 Pet 1:23 cf Jn 3:3–7, Eph 2:11–12 cf Mk 10:29–31/ Rev 5:10, 2 Tim 2:12/ 1 Pet 2:5, 3:9–13

IV '. . . submit . . .' 1 Pet 2:13, 5:5 etc
1 Pet 5:9, 1 Pet 3:9–13/ Acts 8:32–35 cf Mk 14:60 etc (Is 53:7), Jn 13:3–16, 1 Pet 3:1–7/ Jn 15:5, Rev 22:20

V 'My dear friends, do not be surprised . . .' 1 Pet 4:12
Lam 3:23, Jn 10:3/ Mk 10:30/ Lk 12:32, Eph 6:10–20

MOTHERING SUNDAY

PASSIONTIDE

EASTER

Christ died for our sins, . . . that he was raised to life. . .'
1 Cor 15:1–11
1 Cor 11:26 cf Lk 24:30–32. . . 35/ Mk 16:6, Rom 6:9, Heb 7:25/ Jn
15:4/ Lk 24:33–36

3 *Call to worship on Easter morning*   73
'. . . victory through our Lord Jesus Christ!. . .' 1 Cor
15:54–58
Jn 17:3, 20:31/ 1 Cor 15:57/ 1 Cor 15:9–20

4 *Offertory prayer*   73
'. . . God loves . . . one who gives gladly.' 2 Cor 9:7
Jn 19:41, 20:20/ Jn 6:8–13, Mk 1:16–17 etc

5 *Credal prayer*   74
'. . . the one whom Moses wrote about in the book of the
Law and whom the prophets also wrote about. He is
Jesus. . .' Jn 1:45
Gen 1:1, Acts 17:24–31, Ex 6:7, Is 9:6, Jn 3:16, Jn 1:14–18, Jn 13:1,
Phil 2:8, Col 2:12, Rom 6:9/ Jn 20:19, Heb 7:25, Acts 11:12–18, Mt
28:18, Heb 1:3, Acts, 1:11, Mk 13:32/ 2 Cor 5:17, Rev 21:5

6 *The Jews*   75
'. . . Jesus Christ . . . was a descendant of Abraham. . .'
Mt 1:1–17
Rom 9:30–11:12, Mk 8:31–33 etc, Jn 20:20/ Jn 1:12–13, 1 Cor 15:3–9/
Rom 9:30–11:12/ Eph 2:11–22

7 *Light in darkness*   76
'. . . even darkness is not dark for you. . .' Ps 139:7–12
Ps 23:4, Jn 1:4/ Col 3:3, Job 19:23–27a, 1 Cor 6:14/ Jn 20:30–31

8 *Responsive prayers at Easter*   77
'When you pray. . . for something, believe that you have
received it. . .' Mt 11:24
Rom 6:3–4, Jn 20:11–18, 1 Cor 15/ Gal 6:9/ Joel 2:28–29/ Phil 3:8–10a/
Mt 10:32, Rom 6:4/ Jn 14:1–4, 1 Pet 1:3–5/ 1 Cor 15:58

9 *At the beginning of evening worship*   79
'. . . raised to life three days later, he appeared. . .' 1 Cor
15:3–5
Jn 20:24–25/ Lk 24:1–11, Jn 20:1–9/ Mk 16:7/ Lk 24:13–35/ Lk
24:36–40, Jn 20:19–23/ Jn 20:21, Phil 4:7/ Lk 24:29 cf Jn 15:4–5

10 *Opening prayer on the evening of a spring-like Easter Day*   81
'It was late that Sunday evening, and the disciples were
gathered together. . . ' Jn 20:19–21
Mk 16:8, Mk 16:6, Jn 20:20

11 *Petition on Easter evening after reading the Emmaus story*   82
'. . . Jesus . . . walked along with them. . .' Lk 24:13–35

12 *'His joy and ours' – a prayer of commitment*   83
'. . . because of the joy that was waiting for him. . .' Heb
12:2
Heb 12:1–13/ Phil 3:20–21 cf Is 53:11 & AV/ Jn 14:27, Jn 16:33, Jn
15:11, Jn 16:24/ Jn 16:23–24

Low Sunday

13 *The Sunday after Easter – looking in*   84
'. . . When the festival was over, they started back
home. . .' Lk 2:41 . . . 43 . . . 51–52
Lk 9:28–36 cf Lk 9:37–43

14 *The Sunday after Easter – looking out*   85
'As he saw the crowds, his heart was filled with pity . . .'
Mt 9:36–38
Is 1:12–17 cf Is 55:10–11

ASCENSION

1 *Theme prayer*   86
'. . . he was taken up to heaven as they watched . . .' Acts
1:9
Mk 9:2–8 cf 8:27–29, Mt 17:1–8 cf 16:13–20, Lk 9:28–36 cf 9:18–23, Jn
12:12–15 cf 6:15

2 *The King is back in power*   88
'. . . I have been given all authority, in heaven and on
earth . . .' Mt 28:18
Lk 24:50–51, Acts 1:6–11, Jn 3:13 cf Jn 6:38 . . . 62, 2 Cor 4:6, Jn 18:37,
Is 42:2–3, Jn 8:10–11, Lk 7:9 etc, Lk 23:39–43, Lk 7:11–17 cf Jn 11:1–46/
Phil 2:8, Mt 26:50b–56a, Lk 23:34/ Lk 24:2 etc, Jn 20:19, Lk
24:35 . . . 39, Lk 22:19–20, 1 Cor 11:23–26, Jn 16:7 . . . 12–15, Acts
1:8/ Phil 2:9–11 cf Mt 28:18–20/ 2 Cor 5:7, 1 Jn 3:2, 1 Cor 13:12, Jn
16:20, Jn 14:1–3

3 *The transfiguration of man*   89
'. . . when anyone is joined to Christ, he is a new
being . . .' 2 Cor 5:16–17
Jn 3:16/ Is 53:3–12 cf Phil 2:5–16/ Col 3:1, Heb 7:25, Jn 14:12–17, Jn
16:7–15/ Mt 28:18 cf Jn 14:1–4 . . . 27/ Jn 2:4, Jn 9:4, Heb 13:8/ Jn
11:6 . . . 21 . . . 30 . . . 32, Mt 8:20, Mt 18:20, Mt 28:20/ Col 3:1–17/
Jn 4:13–14/ Mt 6:12–15 etc, Mk 12:28–31 etc (cf Deut 6:4 & Lev 19:18),
Jn 15:5, Phil 4:13/ Rom 8:9, Mt 6:9–15/ cf Lk 11:2–13

4 *Royal salute*   90
'. . . We see him now crowned . . .' Heb 2:9
Phil 2:6–11, Phil 3:20–21, Mt 28:18 cf Rev 11:15, Heb 7:25, Rom 8:34,
Acts 1:11 cf Jn 14:3, Rev 22:20

5 *With the children*   91
'. . . continue in the truths which you were taught . . .' 2
Tim 3:14
Jn 3:16, Mt 1 & 2, Lk 1 & 2, Acts 10:38–43 etc, Acts 1:9–11, Jn 14:3, Jn
14:12–17, Jn 16:7–15/ Mk 12:28–31 cf Deut 6:4 & Lev 19:18

6 *Out of sight*   92
'. . . a cloud hid him from their sight . . .; They went back
to Jerusalem, filled with great joy . . .' Acts 1:9–10; Lk 24:52
Acts 1:10–11/ Jn 16:16–19, Lk 24:13–53, Jn 20:11–21:23, Mt 28:9–20,
Acts 1:3–9/ Jn 20:29–31, Jn 17:20–21, Acts 1:4–5 cf Jn 3:8

7 *The Absentee*   93
'. . . it is better for you that I go away . . .'; 'Do not hold on

to me . . .' Jn 16:7 and 20:17
Lk 24:51, Mt 21:18–20 cf Mk 11:12–14 . . . 20–26, Jn 2:15, Mt 27:58 cf
Jn 19:38–40/ Acts 1:9/ Mk 16:6/ Rev 22:20/ Mt 25:40, Jn 14:18, Jn 15:26

8 *To the uplifted Christ*   94
' . . . To him who sits on the throne and to the Lamb, be
praise and honour . . .' Rev 5:6–14
Rev 7:9, Jn 3:14–15/ Jn 3:14–15, Jn 12:32–33/ Mt 25:31–46, Jn 14:3, 1
Thes 4:13–18, Eph 2:5 . . . 8/ Is 6:7 cf Ps 51:7, Rom 12:1–2/ 1 Cor
13:13, 1 Pet 4:17/ Jn 13:4–5 . . . 8 cf Mt 5:16

PENTECOST

1 *Theme prayer*   96
' . . . in a few days you will be baptised with the Holy
Spirit.' Acts 1:5
Gen 1:2/ Jn 14:15–17 . . . 25–26, Jn 15:26–27, Jn 16:7–15, Acts 1:8/
Acts 2:2–3 . . . 14–18 . . . 40–42/ Rom 8:26–39

2 *Picture language*   97
' . . . my Spirit on everyone . . .' Acts 2:1–47 cf Joel 2:28
Mk 1:10, Mt 3:16, Lk 3:22, Jn 1:32/ Jn 3:8/ 1 Kgs 19:12/ Acts 1:4–5, Mt
6:9–13 cf Lk 11:2–4, Rom 8:15, Jn 1:12–13

3 *Whit Sunday morning*   98
'The Helper will come – the Spirit . . .' Jn 15:26
Jn 14:18, Acts 1:9, Acts 2:1–47, Acts 8:1b–40

4 *A family prayer*   100
' . . . the gift my Father promised . . .' Acts 1:4–5
Acts 2:1–14a, Jn 14:18, Jn 15:11, Jn 18:37, Jn 15:13–15, Jn 8:12 cf Mt
5:14–16

5 *An offertory prayer*   100
'Everything . . . in the name of the Lord Jesus . . .' Col
3:17 . . . 23
1 Pet 4:17

6 *Petition*   101
' . . . wait for the gift I told you about . . .' Acts 1:4–5
Heb 10:29, Jn 16:3, Eph 3:16, Lk 11:13

7 *Whit Sunday evening*   102
' . . . the Holy Spirit came down on them, just as on us at
the beginning . . .' Acts 11:15
Mk 6:50 cf Mt 14:27 cf Jn 16:33 cf Jn 14:18, Jn 20:19–22 cf Mt 28:19–20/
Acts 2:2–3/ Acts 2:15/ Acts 2:36/ Mt 18:20, Lk 24:36 cf Mk 6:50 etc & Jn
16:33 (AV)/ Lk 22:19 cf 1 Cor 11:24–25, Lk 24:35

8 *A Whitsun prayer for other times*   104
' . . . some of the Spirit I have given you . . .' Num 11:1–30
Acts 2:1–15/ 2 Chr 24:20, Num 24:2, Judg 3:10 etc, 1 Sam 11:6, 1 Sam
16:13–14, Gen 1:2, Lk 1:35, Mt 3:11–12, Mk 1:10 etc/ Acts 8:14–17,
Acts 10:44 cf 11:15–18, Acts 13:1–3 & 19:1–6/ Joel 2:28–29, Acts 1:4–5,
Jn 15:26 cf 14:6/ Acts 1:8

TRINITY

THANKS AND OFFERING: HARVEST FESTIVAL

ALL SAINTS AND FOR THE CHURCH

Remembrance Sunday

A Statement of Faith   140

INDEX OF MAIN SOURCE REFERENCES

Note Each verse or passage given here is the one which, as the prayer it is attached to evolved, seemed to set its key. But for a particular purpose – for instance in choosing a reading to precede or follow the prayer, one of the secondary references in small type in the Index of Prayers may be found more useful.

INDEX OF THE PLACE OF THE PRAYERS IN WORSHIP[1]

APPROACH

(a) to church with a purpose
  Advent 5, 6
  Christmas 2, 5, 9
  Epiphany 4, 6
  Passiontide 6
  Easter 2, 3, 4
  Trinity 3, 6, 8
  Thanks and Offering (Harvest) 1, 2
  All Saints 4
  Remembrance Sunday 1, 3

(b) thanks, praise and joy
  Christmas 1, 6, 7
  Epiphany 5, 6
  Passiontide 3, 4
  Ascension 2, 4
  Pentecost 2
  Trinity 2, 3
  Thanks and Offering (Harvest) 3
  All Saints 2, 3, 6, 7

(c) the need for pardon
  Advent 2, 3, 7
  Christmas 6
  Epiphany 2
  Passiontide 9
  Trinity 7(I), 7(II)
  Thanks and Offering (Harvest) 2, 3
  All Saints 6

(d) what we believe
  Advent 1
  Christmas 1, 3, 4, 7
  Epiphany 1, 5, 6
  Lent 1, 2, 5, 6
  Passiontide 1, 3, 4
  Easter 1, 2, 3, 5, 9, 10
  Ascension 1, 2, 3, 4, 5
  Pentecost 1, 2, 3, 7
  Trinity 1, 2, 3, 6, 7(I), 7(II), 8
  All Saints 1, 4
  Statement of Faith

FAMILY AWARENESS

(a) all together
  Advent 5
  Trinity 7(I)

(b) thank you, God
  Mothering Sunday 2
  Thanks and Offering (Harvest) 3

(c) living thanks
  Christmas 4
  Trinity 5, 6

(d) the Lord Jesus
  Ascension 5
  Pentecost 4
  Trinity 7(I), 7(II)

(e) think, then pray
  Trinity 7(II)
  Remembrance Sunday 5

[1]For an explanation of this Index, see Introduction, p. 10.

OFFERING

(a) at Communion
Lent **4**

(b) with thanks
Thanks and Offering (Harvest) **4, 5**

(c) of ourselves
Epiphany **4**
Lent **4**
Passiontide **5**
Easter **4**

(d) gifts and givers
Easter **4**
Thanks and Offering (Harvest) **4, 5**

(e) as action
Passiontide **5**
Pentecost **5**
Thanks and Offering (Harvest) **4, 6**

INTERCESSION

(a) about the Church
Advent **4, 6**
Christmas **5, 8**
Lent **1**
Passiontide **8, 11**
Easter **6, 7, 13, 14** (Low Sunday)
Ascension **8**
Pentecost **1, 3, 7, 8**
All Saints **2, 3, 4, 5, 6, 7**

(b) about people
Christmas **8**
Epiphany **1, 3**

Mothering Sunday **1, 3**
Passiontide **7, 8**
Easter **6, 7, 8, 14** (Low Sunday)
Ascension **6**
Remembrance Sunday **2, 4**

(c) about problems
Christmas **5, 8**
Epiphany **3**
Mothering Sunday **1**
Passiontide **8**
Easter **6, 7, 8**

COMMITMENT AND PETITION

(a) as worship begins
Advent **1, 2, 3, 6**
Christmas **4, 5**
Epiphany **2, 4, 6**
Easter **1**
Trinity **6**
All Saints **4**

(b) after readings
Advent **7**
Christmas **4**
Epiphany **1, 2**
Lent **2, 3, 4, 5, 6, 7**(i), **7**(ii), **7**(iii),
    7(iv), **7**(v)
Passiontide **2, 4, 6, 8, 10**
Easter **1, 6, 7, 11, 12**
Ascension **3, 6, 7, 8**
Pentecost **3, 7, 8**
Trinity **4, 5**
All Saints **2, 3, 4**

(c) after hymns
Advent **4**
Christmas **4**
Passiontide **11**
Easter **1**
Pentecost **6**
Trinity **8**

(d) 'Forth in thy name'
Advent **1, 4, 6**
Christmas **9, 10** (New Year)
Epiphany **2, 4, 6**
Lent **1, 2, 3, 5, 6**
Easter **11**
Pentecost **1, 4**
Trinity **5, 8**
Thanks and Offering (Harvest) **2**
All Saints **2, 3, 5, 6**

INDEX OF RELATED HYMNS